Sustainable Wireless Network-on-Chip Architectures

Sustainable Wireless Network-on-Chip Architectures

Jacob Murray

Paul Wettin

Partha Pratim Pande

Behrooz Shirazi

AMSTERDAM • BOSTON • HEIDELBERG • LONDON
NEW YORK • OXFORD • PARIS • SAN DIEGO
SAN FRANCISCO • SINGAPORE • SYDNEY • TOKYO

Morgan Kaufmann is an imprint of Elsevier

Morgan Kaufmann is an imprint of Elsevier
50 Hampshire Street, 5th Floor, Cambridge, MA 02139, USA

Notices
Knowledge and best practice in this field are constantly changing. As new research and experience broaden our understanding, changes in research methods, professional practices, or medical treatment may become necessary.

Practitioners and researchers must always rely on their own experience and knowledge in evaluating and using any information, methods, compounds, or experiments described herein. In using such information or methods they should be mindful of their own safety and the safety of others, including parties for whom they have a professional responsibility.

To the fullest extent of the law, neither the Publisher nor the authors, contributors, or editors, assume any liability for any injury and/or damage to persons or property as a matter of products liability, negligence or otherwise, or from any use or operation of any methods, products, instructions, or ideas contained in the material herein.

British Library Cataloguing-in-Publication Data
A catalogue record for this book is available from the British Library

Library of Congress Cataloging-in-Publication Data
A catalog record for this book is available from the Library of Congress

ISBN: 978-0-12-803625-9

For Information on all Morgan Kaufmann publications
visit our website at https://www.elsevier.com/

Working together
to grow libraries in
developing countries

www.elsevier.com • www.bookaid.org

Publisher: Todd Green
Acquisition Editor: Todd Green
Editorial Project Manager: Lindsay Lawrence
Production Project Manager: Punithavathy Govindaradjane

Typeset by MPS Limited, Chennai, India

CONTENTS

Chapter 1 Introduction 1
The Network-on-Chip Paradigm 1
Traditional NoC Interconnect Topologies...1
Traditional NoC Routing..5
Traditional NoC Backbone 8
References..9

Chapter 2 Current Research Trends and State-of-the-Art NoC
           Designs 11
The Small-World Topology (and Other Irregular Topologies)...........11
Design for Topology-Agnostic Routing for Irregular Networks........14
3D, Optical, and Wireless Integration for NoC................................15
Power- and Temperature-Aware Design Considerations 19
References..20

Chapter 3 Complex Network Inspired NoC Architecture 23
Distance Between Cores (l_{ij}) 23
Frequency of Interaction Between Cores (f_{ij})....................................24
Alpha and Beta...25
f_{ij} for Various Traffic Patterns 26
The Small-World Characteristic 30
References..32
Appendix A.1 L_{ij} Matrix for a 16 Core NoC
with a Tile Floorplan..33
Appendix A.2 F_{ij} Matrix for Uniform Random Traffic 34
Appendix A.3 F_{ij} Matrix for Transpose Traffic................................35
Appendix A.4 F_{ij} Matrix for Hotspot Traffic 36

Chapter 4 Wireless Small-World NoCs..37
Wireless Physical Layer Design 37
Communication and Channelization 40
Topology of Wireless NoCs...42
References..44

Chapter 5 Topology-Agnostic Routing for Irregular Networks............47
A Simple Approach to Topology-Agnostic Routing 47
Routing Strategy for Hierarchical Wireless Small-World Networks...48
Advanced Routing Strategies for Wireless Small-World Networks 49
References..56

Chapter 6 Performance Evaluation and Design Trade-Offs
of Wireless SWNoCs 57
Performance Metrics..60
Optimal Configuration of the SWNoC...60
Throughput of CSWNoC 62
Energy Dissipation for CSWNoC..68
Packet Latency and Energy Dissipation of mSWNoC 69
References..77

Chapter 7 Dynamic Voltage and Frequency Scaling 79
Processor-Level DVFS..79
Network-Level DVFS..81
Performance Evaluation 86
References..105

Chapter 8 Dynamic Thermal Management 107
Temperature-Aware Task Allocation 107
Temperature-Aware Adaptive Routing 110
Experimental Results...113
References..125

Chapter 9 Joint DTM and DVFS Techniques...................................127
Enhanced Routing and Dynamic Thermal Management 127
Joint DTM/DVFS 128
Experimental Results...131
References..141

Chapter 10 Conclusions and Possible Future Explorations.................143
Design of 3D Wireless Small-World NoCs.......................................143
DVFS Pruning..144
Voltage Frequency Island..154
Concluding Remarks 155
References..155

CHAPTER 1

Introduction

THE NETWORK-ON-CHIP PARADIGM

Massive multicore processors are enablers for numerous information and communication technology innovations spanning various domains, including healthcare, defense, entertainment, etc. Continuing progress and integration levels in silicon technologies make possible complete, end-user systems on a single chip in order to meet the growing needs for computation-intensive applications. Clock scaling to meet these needs is not feasible as power and heat become dominant constraints to chip design. As current VLSI technologies can integrate many transistors, parallelism is the key to keeping up with the computational demands. However, the number of cores needed to keep up with the computational demands is drastically increasing.

Chips with ever-increasing cores have been demonstrated by industry. Some examples include Intel's TeraScale processor research program (Held et al., 2006), having developed an 80-core research processor and a 48-core single-chip cloud computer (Vangal et al., 2008; Howard et al., 2010). An Intel 22 nm, 256-core chip has also recently been developed (Chen et al., 2014). Tilera has developed a line of TILE-Gx and TILE-Mx processors with core counts up to 100. As designs with 100s of embedded cores are developed, a need for a platform-based interconnection infrastructure has arisen. As such, the Network-on-Chip (NoC) paradigm has been introduced to provide modularity and regularity via a dedicated infrastructure for interconnections. NoCs have been used in the abovementioned processors and additionally, this paradigm has introduced a new area for research into the many-core architecture domain.

TRADITIONAL NoC INTERCONNECT TOPOLOGIES

Traditionally, few cores integrated on a single chip allow for simple bus interconnect strategies, where one sender broadcasts data onto the bus, and the intended receiver reads the bus line. As the number of cores scales, the bus quickly becomes a bottleneck as more cores are trying to communicate on the bus. While this consists of minimal over-head, network congestion leads to high latency and low throughput. Latency is defined as the amount of time that passes when the sending core sends out data to the point in which the receiving core obtains that data. Throughput is defined as the total amount of data moving at any one given instant of time within the NoC. An example of a 16-core bus network can be seen in Fig. 1.1a. Direct extensions of the bus network include multibus and hierarchical-bus networks (Thepayasuwan et al., 2004). Multiple busses can be added into the

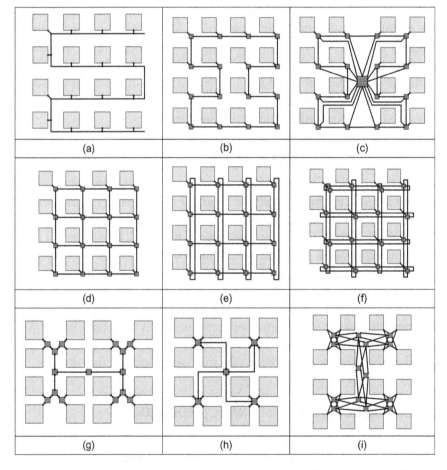

Figure 1.1 Various 16-core traditional NoC interconnect topologies: (a) Bus, (b) ring, (c) star-ring, (d) mesh, (e) torus, (f) folded torus, (g) binary tree, (h) quad tree, and (i) butterfly fat tree.

network so a single core is not able to congest the entire network, allowing additional cores to be able to transfer their data as well.

A continuation of the bus network is the ring and star-ring networks, seen in Fig. 1.1b and c, respectively. For a ring, each core is connected to its own individual network switch and the network switches are connected to two neighbors. In the case of the star-ring an additional central network switch connects to all other switches. The dedicated switch in the star-ring network allows the core to send its data and do other tasks while the network switches take care of data delivery. An insufficiency with the ring network is that the average hop count between cores is relatively high as can be seen in Table 1.1. Hop count is the number of links that data has to traverse before arriving at the destination core from the sending core considering uniform random traffic. The more cores that are inserted into the ring network, on average, the more number of hops it takes to reach any other core. The star-ring network was created to introduce shortcuts into the network to try and reduce the average hop count within the network, reducing the average hop count from 6.2 to 3.8 for a 16-core network, as seen in Table 1.1. However, this requires a very large network switch, with N ports, for an N core network to be built that has to connect to each of the other network switches. Although the central switch reduces the average hop count, it also creates a traffic bottleneck; all of the traffic will try to use this network switch as it creates shortcuts in the network.

Increasing the average number of links per switch can decrease the average hop count of the network. The mesh network produces a regular grid-like structure where each network switch is connected to each of its cardinal neighbors. The average number of links per switch is greater in mesh than that of a ring network, 3:2 for a 16-core network, which can be seen in Table 1.1. A 16-core mesh can be seen in Fig. 1.1d. The mesh layout has been implemented in existing chips and works well as it is easy to construct and scale using a standard processing tile (which includes a processor, cache, and an NoC switch). While it has relatively good throughput, as it is scaled, paths begin to have large number of hops. In a simple example, communicating from one corner of the mesh to another takes $(M-1) + (N-1)$ hops, where M and N are the number of rows and columns in the mesh, respectively. This growth in hop count can be seen in Table 1.1.

Table 1.1 Scalability of Various Traditional NoC Interconnect Topologies

		Bus	Ring	Star-Ring	Mesh	Torus	Folded Torus	Binary Tree	Quad Tree	Butterfly Fat Tree
N = 16	Average number of connections per switch	1	2	4	3	4	4	1.8667	1.6	3.4286
	Average hop count	1	6.2667	3.8667	4.6667	4.1333	4.1333	6.5333	3.6	4.6667
	Total number of switches	N/A	16	17	16	16	16	15	5	14
	Max hop count	1	10	4	8	6	6	8	4	6
	Average link length	16	1	1.5	1	1.5	2	1	1.2	1
	Maximum number of connections per switch	N/A	2	16	4	4	4	3	5	6
N = 32	Average number of connections per switch	1	2	4	3.25	4	4	1.9355	1.8182	3.7333
	Average hop count	1	10.2581	3.9355	6	5.0968	5.0968	8.3226	4.8387	6.3871
	Total number of switches	N/A	32	33	32	32	32	31	11	30
	Max hop count	1	18	4	12	8	8	10	6	8
	Average link length	32	1	2	1	1.625	2	1.0323	1.2381	1.125
	Maximum number of connections per switch	N/A	2	32	4	4	4	3	5	6
N = 64	Average number of connections per switch	1	2	4	3.5	4	4	1.9683	1.9048	3.871
	Average hop count	1	17.9206	3.9683	7.3333	6.0635	6.0635	10.1905	4.8387	8.2222
	Total number of switches	N/A	64	65	64	64	64	63	21	62
	Max hop count	1	34	4	16	10	10	12	6	10
	Average link length	64	1	1.8125	1	1.75	2	1.0909	1.3333	1.1765
	Maximum number of connections per switch	N/A	2	64	4	4	4	3	5	6

Another two topologies that are variations of mesh are the torus and folded torus as can be seen in Fig. 1.1e and f, respectively. In a torus, each switch is not only connected to its cardinal neighbors but also has extra links for each row and column that connects the first and last switch in each row and column, respectively. The folded torus is similar to the torus except that every other switch in a row or column is connected to each other, instead of its direct neighbors. This allows the connections between switches to be uniform in length for the folded torus instead of having a few connections that are physically long like that in a normal torus. Both the torus and folded torus topologies are easy to construct, just like the mesh network. These two networks can be designed using a standard processing tile, but have half the maximum hop count. The reduction in hop count is due to the connections that wrap around in torus, and the connections that can go the length of two hops, compared to a normal mesh, in the folded torus. This can be seen in Table 1.1.

The final category of traditional NoC networks are tree networks, namely, the binary tree, quad tree, and butterfly fat tree which can be seen in Fig. 1.1g–i, respectively. Tree networks are made by connecting multiple cores to each network switch and repeating this pattern until the whole network has been interconnected. For the binary tree and quad tree networks, the goal is to reduce the area overhead of the switches by reducing the number of switches needed, which can be seen in Table 1.1. All tree networks have bottlenecks in the root switches as all traffic needs to move through the root switch to travel to different subtrees within the network. The butterfly fat tree tries to address the bottleneck problem by introducing both multiple root switches and redundant connections between each level of the tree.

TRADITIONAL NoC ROUTING

Routing for traditional NoCs is typically done by using rule-based strategies like X–Y and Up*–Down* routings. Rule-based routing strategies use nominal logic which minimizes the overall area overhead of employing an NoC. However, these rule-based routing strategies come at the cost of causing network congestion. Fig. 1.2a shows an example of X–Y routing in a mesh network.

For this example, data was generated in core 1 whose destination is core 15. Core 1 injects the data into the switch associated with core 1.

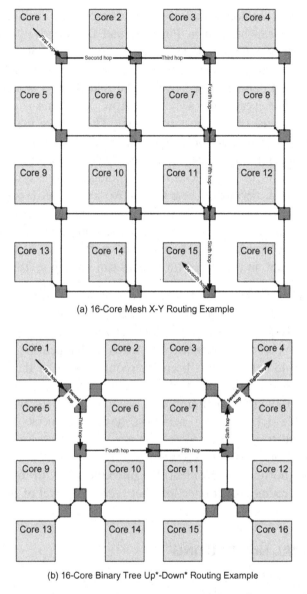

(a) 16-Core Mesh X-Y Routing Example

(b) 16-Core Binary Tree Up*-Down* Routing Example

Figure 1.2 Examples of (a) X−Y routing on a 16-core mesh interconnect, (b) Up*-Down* routing on a 16-core binary tree interconnect.

Once all of the data has been transmitted to the switch, core 1 can start other tasks and not worry about how the data is transported. X−Y routing is typically routed by first matching the data to its corresponding destination column first, then destination row. In this case the destination column is to the right of the first switch. It continues this direction for a total of 2 hops. Once the data is in a switch that is in the same column as the destination, the data will then try to match the destination row. In this example the destination core is below the switch associated with core 3, so the data will move in the downward direction for 3 hops. Once the data is located in the switch associated with core 15, it will deliver the data to that core. A variation on X–Y routing is Y–X routing; data will first try to match the destination row first, followed by destination column. As mentioned earlier, the bigger the network becomes the larger the average hop count becomes in a mesh network. The longer the data has to move through the network to reach its destination, there is a larger chance that there is data that will compete for network resources which in turn will lead to a larger latency before data can be delivered.

Fig. 1.2b shows an example of Up*–Down* routing for tree networks. Data will route up the tree A number of times, where A is a number greater than or equal to zero, until a common subtree switch has been reached. It will then route down the tree B number of times, where B is a number greater than or equal to zero. Once data has begun to move in the downward direction in the tree, it will never use a link in the up direction. For this example, data was generated in core 1 whose destination is core 4. Core 1 injects the data into the first switch which is then routed up the tree for 3 hops until it reaches the root switch. The data then moves down the tree for 4 more hops until it reaches core 4. As mentioned earlier in this chapter, tree networks have a bottleneck problem in the root switch. As the network becomes larger, more traffic will try to use the root switch increasing the average network latency.

Routing in a ring network is typically done by choosing the link that will take the shortest path to get to the destination core. As the network becomes larger, the average hop count increases. Similar to mesh, the longer the data is within the network the more chance it will have for other data to compete for the same network resources, increasing network latency. Comparable to the ring network, routing in the star-ring network will also pick the shortest path; most of the time, this is through the central switch. The star-ring network however has network issues similar to tree networks; the central switch is essentially one giant root switch connected to all the other switches. Almost all data will try to use this central switch creating a bottleneck. This leads to large average network latency.

Many routing variants including fully and partially adaptive routing schemes (Li et al., 2006; Schonwald et al., 2007; Flich, et al., 2012) and compact table-and segment-based routing (Thorup et al., 2001; Flich et al., 2007) have been explored in depth, which provide additional improvements on standard X−Y and Up*−Down* routings. While these exist, one focus of this book is on adopting suitable routing strategies for topology-agnostic networks, which will be explored throughout the following chapters.

TRADITIONAL NoC BACKBONE

As a standard, the NoC paradigm has been used as a scalable interconnection infrastructure for these newly integrated many-core chips. Many advances in NoC research, including power efficiency, reliability, and sustainability, have made it a valid choice as a communication backbone in multicore and many-core chips. Although the existing method of implementing an NoC with planar metal interconnects is a very mature process, it is deficient due to the high latency, significant power consumption, and temperature hotspots arising out of long, multihop wireline paths used in data exchange with scaling technology nodes. Additional issues of physical wire defects and electromigration worsen the reliability of metal interconnects. According to the International Technology Roadmap for Semiconductors, for the longer term, improvements in metal wire characteristics will no longer satisfy performance requirements and new interconnect paradigms are needed. Fig. 1.3 presents how energy dissipated per bit changes as a function

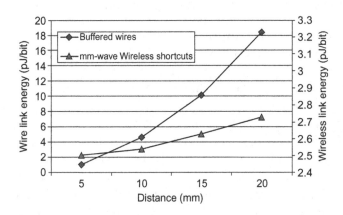

Figure 1.3 Energy/bit versus wire length for a planar metal interconnect.

of length for both wireline and wireless links. From this plot it can be observed that long wireline links require substantial energy to use. Hence, implementation of long-range links beyond a certain length should be implemented using nontraditional link methodologies, such as on-chip photonic links or wireless on-chip channels.

REFERENCES

Chen, G., et al., 2014. A 340 mV-to-0.9 V 20.2 Tb/s source-synchronous hybrid packet/circuit-switched 16 × 16 Network-on-Chip in 22 nm tri-gate CMOS. In: Proceedings of IEEE International Solid-State Circuits Conference. pp. 276−278.

Flich, J., Mejia, A., Lopez, P., Duato, J., 2007. Region-based routing: an efficient routing mechanism to tackle unreliable hardware in Network on Chips. In: First International Symposium on Networks-on-Chip. NOCS 2007, May 7−9, 2007. pp. 183−194.

Flich, J., et al., 2012. A survey and evaluation of topology-agnostic deterministic routing algorithms. IEEE Trans. Parallel Distrib. Syst. 23 (3), 405−425.

Held, J., et al., 2006. From a few cores to many: a tera-scale computing research review, Intel White Paper.

Howard, J., et al., 2010. A 48-core IA-32 message-passing processor with DVFS in 45 nm CMOS. In: Proceedings of the International Solid-State Circuits Conference, February 2010.

Li, M., Zeng, Q.-A., Jone, W.-B., 2006. DyXY: a proximity congestion-aware deadlock-free dynamic routing method for network-on-chip. Proceedings of the 43rd Annual Design Automation Conference (DAC '06). ACM, New York, NY, pp. 849−852.

Schonwald, T., Zimmermann, J., Bringmann, O., Rosenstiel, W., 2007. Fully adaptive fault-tolerant routing algorithm for Network-on-Chip architectures. In: 10th Euromicro Conference on Digital System Design Architectures, Methods and Tools, August 29−31, 2007. DSD 2007. pp. 527−534.

Thepayasuwan, N., et al., 2004. OSIRIS: automated synthesis of flat and hierarchical bus architectures for deep submicron systems on chip. In: Proceedings of the IEEE Computer Society Annual Symposium on VLSI, February 2004. pp. 264−265.

Thorup, M., Zwick, U., 2001. Compact routing schemes. Proceedings of the Thirteenth Annual ACM Symposium on Parallel Algorithms and Architectures (SPAA '01). ACM, New York, NY, pp. 1−10.

Vangal, S.R., et al., 2008. An 80-Tile Sub-100-W TeraFLOPS Processor in 65-nm CMOS. IEEE J. Solid-State Circuits 43 (1), 29−41.

CHAPTER 2

Current Research Trends and State-of-the-Art NoC Designs

THE SMALL-WORLD TOPOLOGY (AND OTHER IRREGULAR TOPOLOGIES)

Traditional NoC topologies, like mesh, are deficient due to the multi-hop nature of the networks. The larger the networks become, the more intermediate hops are needed to communicate data across those networks. This is due to using spatial rules to interconnect the networks, with mesh specifically connecting the nodes based on cardinal neighbors.

Irregular topologies, including small-world, interconnect the network elements regardless of spatial information of the nodes. This allows shortcuts within the network; directly connecting nodes that are physically separated. Many naturally occurring complex networks, such as social networks, the Internet, the brain, as well as microbial colonies, exhibit the small-world property. Specifically, a small-world network is a type of mathematical graph in which most nodes are not direct neighbors of one another, but most nodes can be reached from every other by a small number of hops (Watts and Strogatz, 1998). An example small-world graph can be seen in Fig. 2.1a.

Other well-known irregular topologies are scale-free (Barabasi and Bonabeau, 2003) and Erdős−Rényi (Erdos and Renyi, 1959) topologies which can be seen in Fig. 2.1b and c, respectively. Scale-free networks are considered to be a subset of small-world networks. These are types of mathematical graph in which the number of links originating from a given node exhibits a power law distribution. An Erdős−Rényi network, also known as a random network, is a type of mathematical graph in which nodes can be connected with equal probability, independent of any other link already established within the network.

(a)   (b)

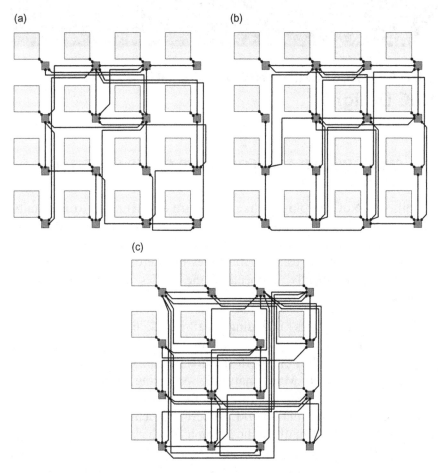

(c)

Figure 2.1 Various 16-core irregular NoC interconnect topologies.

Fig. 2.2 shows three different networks on a scale of how the links interconnect the nodes. On the left of Fig. 2.2 is an Erdős–Rényi network, where the links between nodes are completely random and any two nodes can be connected, independent of existing links or distance between nodes. On the right of Fig. 2.2 is a torus network, where each node is connected to its cardinal neighbors and where the rows and columns wrap around to the start and end of each row or column to ensure that each node has four connections. The network in the middle of Fig. 2.2 is a small-world network where nodes close together are connected, but also, there are short-cuts throughout the network so data can reach any node in a small number of hops. Table 2.1 summarizes the differences of these networks assuming uniform random traffic. Networks with the small-world

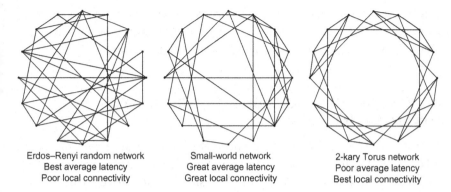

Erdos–Renyi random network
Best average latency
Poor local connectivity

Small-world network
Great average latency
Great local connectivity

2-kary Torus network
Poor average latency
Best local connectivity

Figure 2.2 Network connectivity graph for irregular networks.

Table 2.1 Scalability of Various Irregular NoC Interconnect Topologies		Small-World	Scale-Free	Random
$N = 16$	Average number of connections per switch	4	4	4
	Average hop count	4.4	4.3333	4.2667
	Total number of switches	16	16	16
	Max hop count	6	6	6
	Average link length	1.5913	1.5495	2.1691
	Maximum number of connections per switch	6	6	6
$N = 32$	Average number of connections per switch	4	4	4
	Average hop count	4.4111	4.5	4.7419
	Total number of switches	32	32	32
	Max hop count	6	6	6
	Average link length	2.1487	2.2014	3.2543
	Maximum number of connections per switch	7	7	9
$N = 64$	Average number of connections per switch	4	4	4
	Average hop count	4.7112	4.732	4.8
	Total number of switches	64	64	64
	Max hop count	6	6	6
	Average link length	2.4665	2.8623	4.1208
	Maximum number of connections per switch	7	7	9

property have a very short average path length. This makes small-world graphs interesting for efficient communication with minimal resources.

The trade-off with using irregular topologies is that although the average number of hops between the nodes decreases, the average length of each hop increases. With larger system sizes, the trade-off benefits having a smaller average hop count. Additionally, as the network becomes more complex, a need arises for more complex routing algorithms to ensure the network remains deadlock free.

DESIGN FOR TOPOLOGY-AGNOSTIC ROUTING FOR IRREGULAR NETWORKS

Routing in irregular networks is more complex, because routing methods are needed to be typically topology-agnostic. Hence, it is necessary to investigate suitable routing mechanisms for small-world networks. Routing in irregular networks can be classified into two broad categories, viz., rule- and path-driven strategies (Flitch et al., 2012). Rule-driven routing is typically done by employing a spanning tree for the network. Messages are routed along this spanning tree with specific restrictions to achieve deadlock freedom. Because deadlock freedom is taken into account first for these routing strategies, minimal paths through the network for every source–destination pair cannot be guaranteed (Flitch et al., 2012). Conversely, for path-driven routing, minimal paths between all source–destination pairs are first guaranteed and then deadlock freedom is achieved by restricting portions of traffic from using specific resources such as the virtual channels (Flitch et al., 2012). Generally, routing for path-based techniques use routing tables embedded into each NoC switch. These routing tables can be updated on-the-fly and change due to network conditions such as congested switches as well as being able to adapt to network link failures. However, this can be costly in terms of area overhead for not only the routing tables but also the logic required to update the tables on-the-fly; and is only exacerbated when there are an increasing number of cores. Segment-based routing (Mejia et al., 2006; 2008) can use the advantages of having routing tables. One way to reduce the area overhead of using routing tables is to only store intercluster routing information, once the data has reached the destination cluster the NoC switch will swap to an intracluster routing table to finish the delivery.

These routing algorithms have previously been studied for traditional parallel computing systems where the comparative performance evaluation between multiple routing algorithms is predominantly done in terms of achievable saturation throughput (Flitch et al., 2012; Lysne et al., 2006). Conversely, NoCs in the presence of general-purpose chip multiprocessor benchmarks, such as SPLASH-2 (Woo et al., 1995) and

PARSEC (Bienia, 2011), operate below network saturation and their traffic density varies significantly from one benchmark to the other (Marculescu et al., 2009). Hence, instead of only looking at saturation throughput, we should quantify the associated network latency, energy dissipation, and thermal profiles in presence of frequently used, non-synthetic benchmarks.

3D, OPTICAL, AND WIRELESS INTEGRATION FOR NoC

There are different approaches for creating low-latency, long-range communication channels. Three-dimensional (3D) integration, on-chip photonics, RF, and wireless links have been proposed as radical low-power and low-latency alternatives to the conventional planar wire-based designs. Though all of these methodologies are capable of improving the power and latency characteristics of the traditional NoC, there is need for further investigation to determine their suitability to replace or augment existing metal-based planar multihop NoC architectures.

3D integration addresses the scaling challenge by effectively stacking two-dimensional dies and interconnecting them in the z-dimension. This opens the possibilities to speed up the core communication between levels. The increased communication between cores is accomplished by having smaller footprints, heterogeneous integration, shorter interconnects, lower power dissipation, better core architectures, and increased bandwidth between circuit components. Stacking of layers enables a chip footprint with more functionality that can fit into a smaller space. Using heterogeneous integration, different layers can use different technologies which can be optimized onto the different layers; power optimization for memory can be used for a memory layer while speed optimization can be used for another layer. Due to stacking, the average interconnect length is reduced. This in turn allows for shorter delay when communicating data across the dies. Furthermore, reducing the interconnect length also reduces the power consumption by specifically reducing the parasitic capacitance. Also by stacking the layers, the potential to keep signal on-chip can also reduce power consumption. Adding the vertical dimension adds a physical order of connectivity to offer new design possibilities and core interconnection networks. Finally, 3D integration allows the construction of wide bandwidth busses between the different layers. As they are only using the z-dimension, the area overhead of the wide busses is severely reduced. Wide buses specifically alleviate the memory wall problem which in turn can make chips faster. Research into 3D NoCs can be seen in Chen et al. (2015) and Jabbar et al. (2013).

However, there are many challenges to overcome before 3D integration is widely adopted; specifically, manufacturing cost, manufacturing yield, heat dissipation issues, design complexity, the 3D layer communication overhead, and testing. Currently, manufacturing 3D circuits is very costly due to the technology being new and nontrivial. Breaking down one chip, you now have to manufacture as many dies as you have layers with all the cost associated with building each layer. Not only does each die layer have its own yield but also putting the whole chip together will have its own yield issues. Heat dissipation will be the main challenge to overcome. Heat generated in the middle of the chip layers correlating to thermal hotspots must be carefully managed. The layer communication overhead cannot be disregarded. Cutting a chip into fourths to make a four-layer stack forgets about the area overhead it takes to communicate between the layers. At the 45-nm technology node, the area of a 10 μm by 10 μm through-silicon via (TSVs) is comparable to about 50 gates; this does not include the pads to connect the TSVs, keep out zones needed to build the TSVs, and routing obstacles within the metal layers. Testing, specifically the timing critical paths, will be harder to debug and fix when the timing critical paths go across multiple layers.

On-chip photonics address the scaling challenge by allowing the multiplexing of the core communication medium. Effectively this allows the cores to have an all-to-all network scheme without the long delay overhead usually associated with an all-to-all scheme. This frees up the cores from having to wait to transmit their data while waiting for communication access. Another benefit of using on-chip photonics is the small area overhead of the photonic components, allowing chips to be more compact or enabling chip designers to more efficiently use chip area, not wasting space for communication components. Additionally, communication between the cores is done at the speed of light in an optical waveguide; there are no long wires to charge or discharge, thus increasing the bandwidth of the communication medium. Using optical components also substantially lowers the power dissipation of communication between cores; only dissipating minimal power to inject and receive data from the optical medium, not to move data within the medium. Research into optical NoCs can be seen in Koohi et al. (2010) and Koohi et al. (2011).

However, there are many challenges to overcome before on-chip photonic integration is widely adopted; specifically, silicon-photonic integration, manufacturing cost and yield, temperature sensitivity of the photonic components, design complexity, testing, and laser source integration. Currently, nontraditional methods are used when constructing the photonic layers upon a standard silicon wafer. The integration of the photonic layers is integral to a working photonic chip. Design of the photonic layers will also be critical to photonic chips. The optical waveguides have strict construction rules to allow the optical signal to propagate properly. Also, testing of photonic chips with traditional methods, like bed-of-nails, will not work; new testing methodologies will need to be developed to test the optical components. Finally, integration of the laser source, whether on- or off-chip, needs to be taken into account along with the power dissipation of the laser source.

RF interconnect technologies are very similar to on-chip photonics; however, they use high-frequency waves instead of photons to transmit their data within waveguides. RF interconnect technologies can use current manufacturing technologies to make the routing waveguides which saves in manufacturing time and cost. They can potentially turn multihop paths into single-hop, high-bandwidth paths saving both delay and power dissipation.

However, there are many challenges to overcome before RF interconnect technologies are widely adopted; specifically, waveguide manufacturing, area overhead, transmission length, and testing. Although manufacturing the waveguides can be done with current technology and techniques, the layout design of such waveguides is nontrivial. Depending on the exact frequencies used, the area overhead of the transceivers must be taken into account when designing the chip. The area overhead of the transceivers can be reduced by using higher frequencies; however, this comes at the cost of reducing the transmission length possible within the waveguides. Reducing the transmission length too much can in turn make multihop paths which is the original bottleneck. Also, testing of the RF components become nontrivial, new testing methodologies will be needed to verify that the RF components are working as intended.

Wireless interconnect technologies that do not use waveguides, such as millimeter (mm)-wave metal antennas and carbon nanotube (CNT)-based antennas, can be used to address the scaling core integration issue. The main benefit for both antenna styles is the removal of multi-hop paths between cores; replacing them with high-bandwidth, single-hop links; saving in both delay and power dissipation. Millimeter-wave metal antennas can be manufactured using current manufacturing techniques. They also do not require special waveguide layers to control where the signal propagates. CNT-based antennas can also reduce the area overhead of the wireless transceiver components.

However, there are many challenges to overcome before wireless interconnect technologies can be widely adopted; specifically, manufacturing cost, manufacturing yield, area overhead of the transceivers, integration issues, transceiver design, noisy wireless channels, and testing. The area overhead of the wireless transceivers will need to be considered when designing chips. The manufacturing steps needed to grow the CNT antennas take extra steps to manufacture. Also, the heat needed to grow the antennas can potentially damage the underlying silicon layers. If using more than one channel to transmit data throughout the chip, transceiver design becomes nontrivial. As the wireless medium is shared and is broadcast into the die, the channel can become noisy, which needs careful design considerations and planning. Additionally, new testing methodologies will need to be created to be able to test the accuracy of using the wireless medium.

These emerging interconnect technologies can enable the design of so-called small-world on-chip network architectures, where closely spaced cores will communicate through traditional metal wires, but long-distance communications will be predominantly achieved through high-performance specialized links (Ogras and Marculescu, 2006). Adopting novel architectures inspired by such natural complex networks in conjunction with emerging interconnection technologies will enable design of high-performance and robust multicore chips for the future.

One possible innovative and novel approach is to replace multihop wireline paths in a Network-on-Chip by high-bandwidth, single-hop, long-range wireless links (Ganguly et al., 2011; Deb et al., 2010). The on-chip wireless links facilitate the design of a small-world NoC by enabling one-hop data transfers between distant nodes. However, even these Wireless Networks-on-Chip (WiNoCs) can still exhibit temporal and spatial hotspots among the processing cores and network components. By utilizing long-range wireless links, in addition to reducing interconnect delay and eliminating multihop, long-distance wireline communication, it reduces the energy dissipation as well. However, the overall energy dissipation of the wireless NoC is still dominated by wireline links.

POWER- AND TEMPERATURE-AWARE DESIGN CONSIDERATIONS

Power and heat have become dominant constraints in designing these massive multicore chips. The increasing power consumption is of growing concern due to several reasons, for example, cost, performance, reliability, scalability, and environmental impact. High power consumption not only raises chip temperature and cooling cost but also decreases chip reliability and performance.

As hundreds of cores are integrated in a single chip, designing effective packages for dissipating maximum heat is infeasible (Hanumaiah et al., 2009). Moreover, technology scaling is pushing the limits of affordable cooling, thereby requiring suitable design techniques to reduce peak temperatures. Temperature hotspots witnessed in multicore systems exacerbate the problem of reliability in deep submicron technologies. Thus, addressing thermal concerns at different stages of the design is critical to the success of future generation systems. In this context, dynamic thermal management (DTM) appears as a solution to avoid high spatial and temporal variations among network components, and thereby mitigate local processor and network hotspots. Recent works on DTM (Chaparro et al., 2007) for multicore architectures focus on optimizing the performance of the cores only and explore the design space in the presence of thermal constraints. However, the performance of a multicore chip is also heavily influenced by its overall communication infrastructure.

The link utilization varies depending on the on-chip communication patterns. Tuning the link bandwidth accurately to follow the traffic requirements opens up possibilities of significant power savings. Dynamic voltage and frequency scaling (DVFS) is a well-known technique that enables adjusting the bandwidth of the wireline links by suitably varying their voltage and frequency levels. Consequently, this will enable power savings and lowering of temperature hotspots in specific regions of the chip. The aim is to show how novel NoC architectures with long-range wireless links and DVFS-enabled wireline interconnects lower the energy dissipation of a multicore chip, and consequently help to improve the thermal profile. After addressing the network-level issues, the processing cores are also addressed by implementing DVFS among them as well.

Thermal optimization in the form of DTM techniques also appear as a solution to avoid high spatial and temporal thermal variations and thereby avoid localized hotspots (Chaparro et al., 2007). By implementing new thermal management strategies in conjunction with a dual-level DVFS strategy on a WiNoC should significantly decrease the overall thermal profile while not incurring significant performance penalties. We propose applying a dual-level DTM strategy to simultaneously address processor- and network-level hotspots in WiNoC architectures. We demonstrate that by incorporating a temperature-aware task allocation heuristic to the processing cores, and a dynamic routing strategy to the switches, it is possible to reduce local temperature hotspots in WiNoCs without a significant performance impact. As a final step, we further explore the capabilities of irregular congestion-aware routing strategies coupled with suitable DVFS techniques jointly to further reduce temperatures of the NoC.

REFERENCES

Barabasi, A., Bonabeau, E., 2003. Scale-free networks. Sci. Am. 50−60.

Bienia, C., 2011. Benchmarking Modern Multiprocessors (Ph.D. dissertation). Dept. Computer Science, Princeton Univ., Princeton, NJ.

Chaparro, P., Gonzalez, J., Magklis, G., Qiong, C., Gonzalez, A., 2007. Understanding the thermal implications of multicore architectures. IEEE Trans. Parallel Distrib. Syst. 18 (8), 1055−1065.

Chen, K., et al., 2015. Thermal-aware 3D Network-on-Chip (3D NoC) designs: routing algorithms and thermal management. IEEE Circ. Syst. 45−69.

Deb, S., et al., 2010. Enhancing performance of Network-on-Chip architectures with millimeter-wave wireless interconnects. In: Proceedings of IEEE International Conference on ASAP. pp. 73−80.

Erdos, P., Renyi, A., 1959. On random graphs. Publ. Math. 290−297.

Flich, J., Skeie, T., Mejía, A., Lysne, O., López, P., Robles, A., et al., 2012. A survey and evaluation of topology-agnostic deterministic routing algorithms. IEEE Trans. Parallel Distrib. Syst. 23 (3), 405−425.

Ganguly, A., et al., 2011. Scalable hybrid wireless Network-on-Chip architectures for multi-core systems. IEEE Trans. Comput. 60 (10), 1485−1502.

Hanumaiah, V., Vrudhula, S., Chatha, K.S., 2009. Maximizing performance of thermally constrained multi-core processors by dynamic voltage and frequency control. In: Proceedings of ICCAD. pp. 310−313.

Jabbar, M., et al., 2013. Impact of 3D IC on NoC topologies: a wire delay consideration. In: Proceedings of Euromicro Conference on Digital System Design. pp. 68−72.

Koohi, S., et al., 2010. Scalable architecture for wavelength-switched optical NoC with multicasting capability. In: Proceedings of Euromicro Conference on Digital System Design. pp. 399−403.

Koohi, S., et al., 2011. All-optical wavelength-routed NoC based on a novel hierarchical topology. In: Proceedings of IEEE NOCS. pp. 97−104.

Lysne, O., Skeie, T., Reinemo, S.-A., Theiss, I., 2006. Layered routing in irregular networks. IEEE Trans. Parallel Distrib. Syst. 17 (1), 51−65.

Marculescu, R., Ogras, U.Y., Peh, L.-S., Jerger, N.E., Hoskote, Y., 2009. Outstanding research problems in NoC design: system, microarchitecture, and circuit perspectives. IEEE Trans. Comput. Aided Des. Integr. Circuits Syst. 17 (1), 3−21.

Mejia, A., Flich, J., Duato, J., Reinemo, S.-A., Skeie, T., 2006. Segment-based routing: an efficient fault-tolerant routing algorithm for meshes and tori. In: Proc. IPDPS.

Mejia, A., Flich, J., Duato, J., 2008. On the potentials of segment-based routing for NoCs. In: Proc. ICPP.

Ogras, U.Y., Marculescu, R., 2006. It's a small world after all: NoC performance optimization via long-range link insertion. IEEE Trans. VLSI Syst. 14 (7), 693−706.

Watts, D.J., Strogatz, S.H., 1998. Collective dynamics of 'small-world' networks. Nature 393, 440−442.

Woo, S.C., Ohara, M., Torrie, E., Singh, J.P., Gupta, A., 1995. The SPLASH-2 programs: characterization and methodological considerations. In: Proc. of ISCA. pp. 24−36.

CHAPTER 3

Complex Network Inspired NoC Architecture

A complex network is a network that is connected by nonregular and nontrivial links topologically. There are many naturally occurring complex networks such as the Internet, microbial colonies, cortical interconnects, and social groups to name a few. Theoretical studies in complex networks reveal that certain types of network connectivities are inherently more resilient to failures (Albert and Barabási, 2002). Two such networks are more commonly known as small-world and scale-free networks. The small-world network is a type of network in which most nodes are not directly connected with each other, but can be reached from by using a small number of hops or steps. In contrast to small-world, a scale-free network is a type of network in which the number of links originating from a given node exhibits a power law distribution. It should be noted that scale-free networks are considered to be a subset of small-world networks.

In the small-world NoC (SWNoC) topology, each core is connected to an NoC switch and the switches are interconnected to make a small-world network. The small-world network is established following a power law distribution as shown in (3.1),

$$P(i,j) = \frac{\ell_{ij}^{-\alpha} f_{ij}^{\beta}}{\sum_{\forall i} \sum_{\forall j} \ell_{ij}^{-\alpha} f_{ij}^{\beta}} \tag{3.1}$$

where the probability of establishing a link between two switches, i and j, $P(i,j)$, separated by a Euclidean distance of l_{ij}, is proportional to the distance raised to a finite power (Petermann and De Los Rios, 2005). The frequency of traffic interaction between the cores, f_{ij}, is also factored into (3.1) so that more frequently communicating cores have a higher probability of having a direct link.

DISTANCE BETWEEN CORES (l_{ij})

l_{ij} is the Euclidean distance between two cores, namely i and j. The distance is obtained by considering a tile-based floor plan of the cores

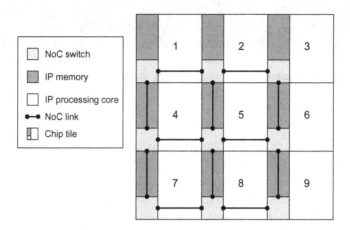

Figure 3.1 Example of 3 × 3 NoC tile floor plan.

on the die. Each tile contains an IP, made up of a processing core and its associated memory, and an NoC network switch. l_{ij} is then the measured distance between the two NoC network switches, normalized against the distance between the shortest directly neighboring NoC network switches. This can be seen in Fig. 3.1, for a 3×3 network. For example, if each tile is a $10\,\mu m \times 10\,\mu m$ square, then $l_{1,9}$ can be calculated to be 2.8284 as seen in (3.2).

$$\ell_{1,9} = \frac{\sqrt{((20\,\mu m)^2 + (20\,\mu m)^2)}}{10\,\mu m} = \frac{\sqrt{800\,\mu m^2}}{10\,\mu m} = \frac{28.28427}{10} = 2.82842 = \sqrt{8}$$

(3.2)

Appendix A.1 shows the l_{ij} matrix for a 16-core system size. l_{ij} can also be made for nonuniform tile sizes.

FREQUENCY OF INTERACTION BETWEEN CORES (f_{ij})

The frequency f_{ij} is expressed as the percentage of traffic generated from core i that is destined to core j. This frequency distribution is based on the particular application mapped to the overall SWNoC and is hence set prior to link insertion. Therefore, the a priori knowledge of the traffic pattern can be used to establish the topology with a correlation between traffic distribution across the NoC and network configuration as in Bogdan and Marculescu (2007). Using the a priori knowledge of the traffic can optimize the network architecture for nonuniform traffic scenarios. For example, if a chip was designed to be used for weather prediction, the amount of traffic each core sends to neighboring cores would not be uniform. Utilizing f_{ij} is only advantageous if the chip is designed to be application specific, if the chip is made to be more general purpose either by removing f_{ij} from (3.1) or by setting β to 0 will ensure that the network is made regardless of any traffic pattern.

ALPHA AND BETA

The parameters, α and β, govern the nature of connectivity and significance of the traffic pattern on the topology, respectively. Alpha governs the nature of the connectivity for the network. In particular, as α increases, the network becomes very locally connected with few or even no long range links, similar to that of a cellular automata-based topology. Whereas, if α were zero, an ideal small-world network would be generated following the Watts–Strogatz model (Zhang et al., 2007) with long-range shortcuts virtually independent of the distance between the cores. To ensure the small-world characteristic, it has been shown in Petermann and De Los Rios (2005) that α should be less than $D + 1$, D being the dimension of the network. Similar to the small-world network, a scale-free network is defined as a network with a power law distribution of links. It was shown in Choromański et al. (2013) that α typically lies within the range $2 < \alpha < 3$.

Beta determines the significance in which the network traffic determines the network connectivity. A lower value of β implies a higher probability of establishing direct links between switches with higher traffic exchange. When β is zero, f_{ij}^{β} becomes 1 making l_{ij} the only determining factor of $P(i,j)$. Both of these parameters, α and β, can be considered as design knobs that may be tuned for a particular application to generate optimized network architectures depending on floor plan and traffic.

Several examples are demonstrated in the following sections for three different traffic scenarios, namely, uniform random, transpose, and hotspot. The destination cores 2, 7, and 16 were picked semi-randomly to highlight some of the features for the different traffic scenarios which are explained below. The locations of these destination cores can be seen in Figs. 3.2–3.4. α was chosen to be 1.8 (Petermann and De Los Rios, 2005) and β was chosen to be 1 to use an unmodified percentage of traffic to determine the network connectivity.

f_{ij} FOR VARIOUS TRAFFIC PATTERNS

Uniform Random Traffic

For uniform random traffic, as the name implies, each core has an equal probability to communicate with every other core. The full f_{ij} matrix for uniform random traffic can be seen in Appendix A.2 and a partial f_{ij} matrix can be seen in (3.3).

$$f_{5,j_{uniform}} = \begin{bmatrix} \frac{1}{15} & \frac{1}{15} & \frac{1}{15} & \frac{1}{15} & 0 & \frac{1}{15} & \frac{1}{15} & \frac{1}{15} \\ \frac{1}{15} & \frac{1}{15} & \frac{1}{15} & \frac{1}{15} & \frac{1}{15} & \frac{1}{15} & \frac{1}{15} & \frac{1}{15} \end{bmatrix} \tag{3.3}$$

Having uniform random traffic essentially nullifies the f_{ij} factor in $P(i,j)$ and makes $P(i,j)$ only upon the distance between two cores. Eqs. (3.4)–(3.6) are examples of determining $P(i,j)$ for uniform random traffic.

$$P(5,2)_{uniform} = \frac{\ell_{5,2}^{-1.8} f_{5,2}^1}{\sum_{\forall i} \sum_{\forall j} \ell_{ij}^{-\alpha} f_{ij}^{\beta}} = \frac{\sqrt{2}^{-1.8} \frac{1}{15}}{6.4896} = \frac{0.03573}{6.4896} = 0.005505 \tag{3.4}$$

$$P(5,7)_{uniform} = \frac{\ell_{5,7}^{-1.8} f_{5,7}^1}{\sum_{\forall i} \sum_{\forall j} \ell_{ij}^{-\alpha} f_{ij}^{\beta}} = \frac{2^{-1.8} \frac{1}{15}}{6.4896} = \frac{0.01914}{6.4896} = 0.00295 \tag{3.5}$$

$$P(5,16)_{uniform} = \frac{\ell_{5,16}^{-1.8} f_{5,16}^1}{\sum_{\forall i} \sum_{\forall j} \ell_{ij}^{-\alpha} f_{ij}^{\beta}} = \frac{\sqrt{13}^{-1.8} \frac{1}{15}}{6.4896} = \frac{0.006628}{6.4896} = 0.001021 \tag{3.6}$$

As core 16 is the farthest from core 5, it also has the lowest probability of having a connection made within the network, 0.1021%; whereas core 2 is the closest to core 5 and has a probability of 0.5505% of having a connection. Core 7 has a probability of 0.295% to be connected to core 5. A 16-core SWNoC using the uniform random f_{ij} can be seen in Fig. 3.2.

Transpose Traffic

Transpose traffic is a pattern of traffic where each core communicates 90% of its traffic to the location reflected along the main diagonal of

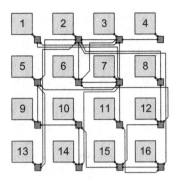

Figure 3.2 Example of 16-core SWNoC with uniform random f_{ij}.

the network, the remaining 10% of the traffic is uniform random. Cores that do not reflect across the main diagonal to another core and cores along the main diagonal keep their traffic as uniform random. The full f_{ij} matrix for transpose traffic can be seen in Appendix A.3 and a partial f_{ij} matrix can be seen in (3.7).

$$f_{5,j\text{transpose}} = \begin{bmatrix} \dfrac{1}{140} & \dfrac{126}{140} & \dfrac{1}{140} & \dfrac{1}{140} & 0 & \dfrac{1}{140} & \dfrac{1}{140} & \dfrac{1}{140} \\[2mm] \dfrac{1}{140} & \dfrac{1}{140} & \dfrac{1}{140} & \dfrac{1}{140} & \dfrac{1}{140} & \dfrac{1}{140} & \dfrac{1}{140} & \dfrac{1}{140} \end{bmatrix} \quad (3.7)$$

Eqs. (3.8)–(3.10) are examples of determining $P(i,j)$ for the transpose traffic.

$$P(5,2)_{\text{transpose}} = \frac{\ell_{5,2}^{-1.8} f_{5,2}^{1}}{\sum_{\forall i}\sum_{\forall j}\ell_{ij}^{-\alpha}f_{ij}^{\beta}} = \frac{\sqrt{2}^{-1.8}\frac{126}{140}^{1}}{3.9701} = \frac{0.4823}{3.9701} = 0.1215 \quad (3.8)$$

$$P(5,7)_{\text{transpose}} = \frac{\ell_{5,7}^{-1.8} f_{5,7}^{1}}{\sum_{\forall i}\sum_{\forall j}\ell_{ij}^{-\alpha}f_{ij}^{\beta}} = \frac{2^{-1.8}\frac{1}{140}^{1}}{3.9701} = \frac{0.002051}{3.9701} = 0.0005167$$

$$(3.9)$$

$$P(5,16)_{\text{transpose}} = \frac{\ell_{5,16}^{-1.8} f_{5,16}^{1}}{\sum_{\forall i}\sum_{\forall j}\ell_{ij}^{-\alpha}f_{ij}^{\beta}} = \frac{\sqrt{13}^{-1.8}\frac{1}{140}^{1}}{3.9701} = \frac{0.0007101}{3.9701} = 0.0001789$$

$$(3.10)$$

As core 2 is both the closest core to core 5 and is also the core reflected along the main diagonal the probability of having a connection between

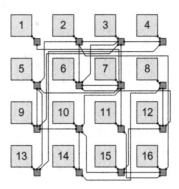

Figure 3.3 Example of 16-core SWNoC with transpose f_{ij}.

these two cores is high, 12.15%. Again as core 16 is the furthest from core 5 and has a lower percentage of traffic, the probability of having a connection is low, 0.01789%. Core 7 has a probability of 0.05167%. A 16-core SWNoC using the transpose f_{ij} can be seen in Fig. 3.3.

Hotspot Traffic

For the hotspot traffic, every core sends a percentage of all its traffic to a particular core. In this example, every core sends 20% of its traffic to core 7. The other 80% of the traffic is uniform random. The full f_{ij} matrix for transpose traffic can be seen in Appendix A.4 and a partial f_{ij} matrix can be seen in (3.11).

$$f_{5,j_{hotspot}} = \begin{bmatrix} \frac{2}{35} & \frac{2}{35} & \frac{2}{35} & \frac{2}{35} & 0 & \frac{2}{35} & \frac{7}{35} & \frac{2}{35} \\ \frac{2}{35} & \frac{2}{35} & \frac{2}{35} & \frac{2}{35} & \frac{2}{35} & \frac{2}{35} & \frac{2}{35} & \frac{2}{35} \end{bmatrix} \quad (3.11)$$

Eqs. (3.12)–(3.14) are examples of determining $P(i,j)$ for the hotspot traffic.

$$P(5,2)_{hotspot} = \frac{\ell_{5,2}^{-1.8} f_{5,2}^{1}}{\sum_{\forall i}\sum_{\forall j}\ell_{ij}^{-\alpha}f_{ij}^{\beta}} = \frac{\sqrt{2}^{-1.8}\frac{2}{35}^{1}}{6.4188} = \frac{0.03062}{6.4188} = 0.004771$$

$$(3.12)$$

$$P(5,7)_{hotspot} = \frac{\ell_{5,7}^{-1.8} f_{5,7}^{1}}{\sum_{\forall i}\sum_{\forall j}\ell_{ij}^{-\alpha}f_{ij}^{\beta}} = \frac{2^{-1.8}\frac{7}{35}^{1}}{6.4188} = \frac{0.05743}{6.4188} = 0.008948 \quad (3.13)$$

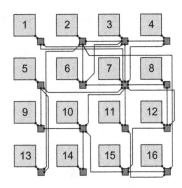

Figure 3.4 Example of 16-core SWNoC with hotspot f_{ij}.

$$P(5,16)_{\text{hotspot}} = \frac{\ell_{5,16}^{-1.8} f_{5,16}^1}{\sum_{\forall i} \sum_{\forall j} \ell_{ij}^{-\alpha} f_{ij}^{\beta}} = \frac{\sqrt{13}^{-1.8} \frac{2}{35}^1}{6.4188} = \frac{0.005681}{6.4188} = 0.000885$$

$$(3.14)$$

Even though core 2 is closer to core 5, core 7 has a higher percentage of core 5's traffic and hence has a higher probability of having a connection. Core 7 and core 2 have a probability of being connected to core 5 by 0.8948% and 0.4771%, respectively. Just like in the other traffic scenarios as core 16 is the furthest away from core 5, it has the lowest probability of being connected to core 5 for these examples, 0.0885%. A 16-core SWNoC using the hotspot f_{ij} can be seen in Fig. 3.4.

Benchmark Suites

The prior example f_{ij} matrices are all generated from synthetic traffics. Many real workload benchmark suites exist, and throughout this book, we explore two such benchmark suites, SPLASH-2 (Woo et al., 1995) and PARSEC (Bienia, 2011). As an example, one such benchmark, CANNEAL from the PARSEC suite, has a partial f_{ij} matrix that can be seen in (3.15).

$$f_{5,j\text{CANNEAL}} = \begin{bmatrix} \frac{760}{7450} & \frac{150}{7450} & \frac{470}{7450} & \frac{840}{7450} & 0 & \frac{630}{7450} & \frac{710}{7450} & \frac{600}{7450} \\ \frac{620}{7450} & \frac{470}{7450} & \frac{460}{7450} & \frac{430}{7450} & \frac{120}{7450} & \frac{310}{7450} & \frac{290}{7450} & \frac{590}{7450} \end{bmatrix}$$

$$(3.15)$$

Eqs. (3.16) and (3.17) are examples of determining $P(i,j)$ for the CANNEAL traffic.

$$P(5,2)_{\text{CANNEAL}} = \frac{\ell_{5,2}^{-1.8} f_{5,2}^{1}}{\sum_{\forall i} \sum_{\forall j} \ell_{ij}^{-\alpha} f_{ij}^{\beta}} = \frac{\sqrt{2}^{-1.8} \frac{150}{7450}^{1}}{6.4188} = \frac{0.01079}{6.4188} = 0.001681$$

(3.16)

$$P(5,7)_{\text{CANNEAL}} = \frac{\ell_{5,2}^{-1.8} f_{5,2}^{1}}{\sum_{\forall i} \sum_{\forall j} \ell_{ij}^{-\alpha} f_{ij}^{\beta}} = \frac{2^{-1.8} \frac{710}{7450}^{1}}{6.4188} = \frac{0.01079}{6.4188} = 0.004264$$

(3.17)

Even though core 2 is closer to core 5, core 7 has a higher percentage of core 5's traffic and hence has a higher probability of having a connection. Core 2 and core 7 have a probability of being connected to core 5 by 0.1681% and 0.4264%, respectively.

THE SMALL-WORLD CHARACTERISTIC

A measure to determine if a network has the small-world characteristic, S, is proposed in Humphries and Gurney (2008) as (3.18).

$$S = \frac{\frac{C}{C_{\text{rand}}}}{\frac{L}{L_{\text{rand}}}}$$

(3.18)

L and C are the characteristic path length and clustering coefficient of the network, respectively. L_{rand} and C_{rand} are the same quantities of a randomly constructed Erdos–Renyi graph, respectively, with the same number of nodes and links as the tested network. L is simply the average shortest path length for the entire network as seen in (3.19).

$$L = \frac{1}{n} \sum_{\forall i} L_i = \frac{1}{n} \sum_{\forall i} \frac{\sum_{\forall j, j \neq i} d_{ij}}{n-1}$$

(3.19)

The shortest path length between two cores i and j, d_{ij}, can be written like (3.20), where g_{ij} is the geodesic path between core i and j, and a_{ij} is the connection status between cores i and j.

$$d_{ij} = \sum_{a_{uv} \in g_{ij}} a_{uv}$$

(3.20)

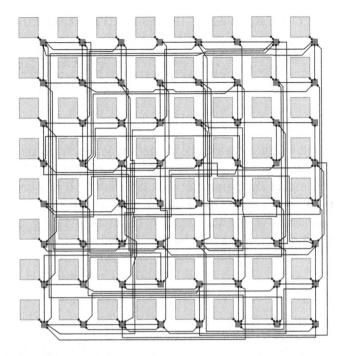

Figure 3.5 Example of 64-core SWNoC.

a_{ij} is equal to 1 if core i is connected to core j and a_{ij} is equal to 0 if core i is not connected to core j as seen in (3.21).

$$a_{ij} = \begin{cases} 1 & \text{if core } i \text{ is connected to core } j \\ 0 & \text{otherwise} \end{cases} \quad (3.21)$$

C is the number of shared edges that core i has with its neighbors divided by the degree of core i, k_i as seen in (3.22).

$$C = \frac{1}{n}\sum_{\forall i} \quad C_i = \frac{1}{n}\sum_{\forall i} \frac{2t_i}{k_i(k_i - 1)} \quad (3.22)$$

The number of shared edges that core i has with its neighbors is simply the number of triangles around core i, t_i, as seen in (3.23). A triangle around core i is defined as two other cores, j and k, are both connected to core i as well as being connected to each other directly. k_i is determined by the number of connections that core i has as seen in (3.24).

$$t_i = \frac{1}{2}\sum_{\forall j \forall h} a_{ij}a_{ih}a_{jh} \quad (3.23)$$

$$k_i = \sum_{\forall j} a_{ij} \quad (3.24)$$

Modifying (3.18) to include (3.19) and (3.22) makes (3.25).

$$
S = \frac{\frac{C}{C_{\text{rand}}}}{\frac{L}{L_{\text{rand}}}} = \frac{\frac{\sum_{\forall i} \frac{2t_i}{k_i(k_i - 1)}}{C_{\text{rand}}}}{\frac{\sum_{\forall i} \frac{\sum_{\forall j, i \neq j} d_{ij}}{n-1}}{L_{\text{rand}}}} = \frac{L_{\text{rand}}}{C_{\text{rand}}} \sum_{\forall i} \frac{(n-1)}{k_i(k_i - 1)} \sum_{\forall j, i \neq j} \frac{\sum_{\forall h, i \neq h, j \neq h} a_{ij} a_{ih} a_{jh}}{\sum_{a_{uv} \in g_{ij}} a_{uv}}
$$

$$(3.25)$$

For a small-world network, the clustering parameter is much larger than that of a random network while the average path length is similar. This makes the parameter S larger than 1. It has been shown in Humphries and Gurney (2008) that many real networks have small-world characteristic if the quantity S is larger than 1. Fig. 3.5 shows an example 64-core network that has $S = 1.7492$.

REFERENCES

Albert, R., Barabási, A.-L., 2002. Statistical mechanics of complex networks. Rev. Mod. Phys. 74, 47–97.

Bienia, C., 2011. Benchmarking Modern Multiprocessors (Ph.D. dissertation). Princeton Univ., Princeton, NJ.

Bogdan, P., Marculescu, R., 2007. Quantum-like effects in network-on-chip buffers behavior. In: Proceedings of DAC. pp. 266–267.

Choromański, K., Matuszak, M., MiçKisz, J., 2013. Scale-free graph with preferential attachment and evolving internal vertex structure. J. Stat. Phys. 151 (6), 1175.

Humphries, M.D., Gurney, K., 2008. Network 'small-world-ness': a quantitative method for determining canonical network equivalence. PLoS One 3 (4).

Petermann, T., De Los Rios, P., 2005. Spatial small-world networks: a wiring cost perspective. arXiv:cond-mat/0501420v2.

Woo, S.C., Ohara, M., Torrie, E., Singh, J.P., Gupta, A., 1995. The SPLASH-2 programs: characterization and methodological considerations. In: Proc. of ISCA. pp. 24–36.

Zhang, Y.P., Chen, Z.M., Sun, M., 2007. Propagation mechanisms of radio waves over intra-chip channels with integrated antennas: frequency-domain measurements and time-domain analysis. IEEE Trans. Antennas Propag. 55 (10), 2900–2906.

APPENDIX A.1 L_{ij} MATRIX FOR A 16 CORE NoC WITH A TILE FLOORPLAN

$$\ell_{ij} = \begin{bmatrix}
0 & 1 & 2 & 3 & 1 & \sqrt{2} & \sqrt{5} & \sqrt{10} & 2 & \sqrt{5} & \sqrt{8} & \sqrt{13} & 3 & \sqrt{10} & \sqrt{13} & \sqrt{18} \\
1 & 0 & 1 & 2 & \sqrt{2} & 1 & \sqrt{2} & \sqrt{5} & \sqrt{5} & 2 & \sqrt{5} & \sqrt{8} & \sqrt{10} & 3 & \sqrt{10} & \sqrt{13} \\
2 & 1 & 0 & 1 & \sqrt{5} & \sqrt{2} & 1 & \sqrt{2} & \sqrt{8} & \sqrt{5} & 2 & \sqrt{5} & \sqrt{13} & \sqrt{10} & 3 & \sqrt{10} \\
3 & 2 & 1 & 0 & \sqrt{10} & \sqrt{5} & \sqrt{2} & 1 & \sqrt{13} & \sqrt{8} & \sqrt{5} & 2 & \sqrt{18} & \sqrt{13} & \sqrt{10} & 3 \\
1 & \sqrt{2} & \sqrt{5} & \sqrt{10} & 0 & 1 & 2 & 3 & 1 & \sqrt{2} & \sqrt{5} & \sqrt{10} & 2 & \sqrt{5} & \sqrt{8} & \sqrt{13} \\
\sqrt{2} & 1 & \sqrt{2} & \sqrt{5} & 1 & 0 & 1 & 2 & \sqrt{2} & 1 & \sqrt{2} & \sqrt{5} & \sqrt{5} & 2 & \sqrt{5} & \sqrt{8} \\
\sqrt{5} & \sqrt{2} & 1 & \sqrt{2} & 2 & 1 & 0 & 1 & \sqrt{5} & \sqrt{2} & 1 & \sqrt{2} & \sqrt{8} & \sqrt{5} & 2 & \sqrt{5} \\
\sqrt{10} & \sqrt{5} & \sqrt{2} & 1 & 3 & 2 & 1 & 0 & \sqrt{10} & \sqrt{5} & \sqrt{2} & 1 & \sqrt{13} & \sqrt{8} & \sqrt{5} & 2 \\
2 & \sqrt{5} & \sqrt{8} & \sqrt{13} & 1 & \sqrt{2} & \sqrt{5} & \sqrt{10} & 0 & 1 & 2 & 3 & 1 & \sqrt{2} & \sqrt{5} & \sqrt{10} \\
\sqrt{5} & 2 & \sqrt{5} & \sqrt{8} & \sqrt{2} & 1 & \sqrt{2} & \sqrt{5} & 1 & 0 & 1 & 2 & \sqrt{2} & 1 & \sqrt{2} & \sqrt{5} \\
\sqrt{8} & \sqrt{5} & 2 & \sqrt{5} & \sqrt{5} & \sqrt{2} & 1 & \sqrt{2} & 2 & 1 & 0 & 1 & \sqrt{5} & \sqrt{2} & 1 & \sqrt{2} \\
\sqrt{13} & \sqrt{8} & \sqrt{5} & 2 & \sqrt{10} & \sqrt{5} & \sqrt{2} & 1 & 3 & 2 & 1 & 0 & \sqrt{10} & \sqrt{5} & \sqrt{2} & 1 \\
3 & \sqrt{10} & \sqrt{13} & \sqrt{18} & 2 & \sqrt{5} & \sqrt{8} & \sqrt{13} & 1 & \sqrt{2} & \sqrt{5} & \sqrt{10} & 0 & 1 & 2 & 3 \\
\sqrt{10} & 3 & \sqrt{10} & \sqrt{13} & \sqrt{5} & 2 & \sqrt{5} & \sqrt{8} & \sqrt{2} & 1 & \sqrt{2} & \sqrt{5} & 1 & 0 & 1 & 2 \\
\sqrt{13} & \sqrt{10} & 3 & \sqrt{10} & \sqrt{8} & \sqrt{5} & 2 & \sqrt{5} & \sqrt{5} & \sqrt{2} & 1 & \sqrt{2} & 2 & 1 & 0 & 1 \\
\sqrt{18} & \sqrt{13} & \sqrt{10} & 3 & \sqrt{13} & \sqrt{8} & \sqrt{5} & 2 & \sqrt{10} & \sqrt{5} & \sqrt{2} & 1 & 3 & 2 & 1 & 0
\end{bmatrix}$$

APPENDIX A.2 F_{ij} MATRIX FOR UNIFORM RANDOM TRAFFIC

$$f_{ij\,uniformrandom} = \begin{bmatrix}
0 & \frac{1}{15} & \frac{1}{15} & \frac{1}{15} & \frac{1}{15} & \frac{1}{15} & \frac{1}{15} & \frac{1}{15} & \frac{1}{15} & \frac{1}{15} & \frac{1}{15} & \frac{1}{15} & \frac{1}{15} & \frac{1}{15} & \frac{1}{15} & \frac{1}{15} \\
\frac{1}{15} & 0 & \frac{1}{15} & \frac{1}{15} & \frac{1}{15} & \frac{1}{15} & \frac{1}{15} & \frac{1}{15} & \frac{1}{15} & \frac{1}{15} & \frac{1}{15} & \frac{1}{15} & \frac{1}{15} & \frac{1}{15} & \frac{1}{15} & \frac{1}{15} \\
\frac{1}{15} & \frac{1}{15} & 0 & \frac{1}{15} & \frac{1}{15} & \frac{1}{15} & \frac{1}{15} & \frac{1}{15} & \frac{1}{15} & \frac{1}{15} & \frac{1}{15} & \frac{1}{15} & \frac{1}{15} & \frac{1}{15} & \frac{1}{15} & \frac{1}{15} \\
\frac{1}{15} & \frac{1}{15} & \frac{1}{15} & 0 & \frac{1}{15} & \frac{1}{15} & \frac{1}{15} & \frac{1}{15} & \frac{1}{15} & \frac{1}{15} & \frac{1}{15} & \frac{1}{15} & \frac{1}{15} & \frac{1}{15} & \frac{1}{15} & \frac{1}{15} \\
\frac{1}{15} & \frac{1}{15} & \frac{1}{15} & \frac{1}{15} & 0 & \frac{1}{15} & \frac{1}{15} & \frac{1}{15} & \frac{1}{15} & \frac{1}{15} & \frac{1}{15} & \frac{1}{15} & \frac{1}{15} & \frac{1}{15} & \frac{1}{15} & \frac{1}{15} \\
\frac{1}{15} & \frac{1}{15} & \frac{1}{15} & \frac{1}{15} & \frac{1}{15} & 0 & \frac{1}{15} & \frac{1}{15} & \frac{1}{15} & \frac{1}{15} & \frac{1}{15} & \frac{1}{15} & \frac{1}{15} & \frac{1}{15} & \frac{1}{15} & \frac{1}{15} \\
\frac{1}{15} & \frac{1}{15} & \frac{1}{15} & \frac{1}{15} & \frac{1}{15} & \frac{1}{15} & 0 & \frac{1}{15} & \frac{1}{15} & \frac{1}{15} & \frac{1}{15} & \frac{1}{15} & \frac{1}{15} & \frac{1}{15} & \frac{1}{15} & \frac{1}{15} \\
\frac{1}{15} & \frac{1}{15} & \frac{1}{15} & \frac{1}{15} & \frac{1}{15} & \frac{1}{15} & \frac{1}{15} & 0 & \frac{1}{15} & \frac{1}{15} & \frac{1}{15} & \frac{1}{15} & \frac{1}{15} & \frac{1}{15} & \frac{1}{15} & \frac{1}{15} \\
\frac{1}{15} & \frac{1}{15} & \frac{1}{15} & \frac{1}{15} & \frac{1}{15} & \frac{1}{15} & \frac{1}{15} & \frac{1}{15} & 0 & \frac{1}{15} & \frac{1}{15} & \frac{1}{15} & \frac{1}{15} & \frac{1}{15} & \frac{1}{15} & \frac{1}{15} \\
\frac{1}{15} & \frac{1}{15} & \frac{1}{15} & \frac{1}{15} & \frac{1}{15} & \frac{1}{15} & \frac{1}{15} & \frac{1}{15} & \frac{1}{15} & 0 & \frac{1}{15} & \frac{1}{15} & \frac{1}{15} & \frac{1}{15} & \frac{1}{15} & \frac{1}{15} \\
\frac{1}{15} & \frac{1}{15} & \frac{1}{15} & \frac{1}{15} & \frac{1}{15} & \frac{1}{15} & \frac{1}{15} & \frac{1}{15} & \frac{1}{15} & \frac{1}{15} & 0 & \frac{1}{15} & \frac{1}{15} & \frac{1}{15} & \frac{1}{15} & \frac{1}{15} \\
\frac{1}{15} & \frac{1}{15} & \frac{1}{15} & \frac{1}{15} & \frac{1}{15} & \frac{1}{15} & \frac{1}{15} & \frac{1}{15} & \frac{1}{15} & \frac{1}{15} & \frac{1}{15} & 0 & \frac{1}{15} & \frac{1}{15} & \frac{1}{15} & \frac{1}{15} \\
\frac{1}{15} & \frac{1}{15} & \frac{1}{15} & \frac{1}{15} & \frac{1}{15} & \frac{1}{15} & \frac{1}{15} & \frac{1}{15} & \frac{1}{15} & \frac{1}{15} & \frac{1}{15} & \frac{1}{15} & 0 & \frac{1}{15} & \frac{1}{15} & \frac{1}{15} \\
\frac{1}{15} & \frac{1}{15} & \frac{1}{15} & \frac{1}{15} & \frac{1}{15} & \frac{1}{15} & \frac{1}{15} & \frac{1}{15} & \frac{1}{15} & \frac{1}{15} & \frac{1}{15} & \frac{1}{15} & \frac{1}{15} & 0 & \frac{1}{15} & \frac{1}{15} \\
\frac{1}{15} & \frac{1}{15} & \frac{1}{15} & \frac{1}{15} & \frac{1}{15} & \frac{1}{15} & \frac{1}{15} & \frac{1}{15} & \frac{1}{15} & \frac{1}{15} & \frac{1}{15} & \frac{1}{15} & \frac{1}{15} & \frac{1}{15} & 0 & \frac{1}{15} \\
\frac{1}{15} & \frac{1}{15} & \frac{1}{15} & \frac{1}{15} & \frac{1}{15} & \frac{1}{15} & \frac{1}{15} & \frac{1}{15} & \frac{1}{15} & \frac{1}{15} & \frac{1}{15} & \frac{1}{15} & \frac{1}{15} & \frac{1}{15} & \frac{1}{15} & 0
\end{bmatrix}$$

APPENDIX A.3 F_{ij} MATRIX FOR TRANSPOSE TRAFFIC

$$
f_{ij\,transpose} =
\begin{bmatrix}
0 & \frac{1}{15} & \frac{1}{15} & \frac{1}{15} & \frac{1}{15} & \frac{1}{15} & \frac{1}{15} & \frac{1}{15} & \frac{1}{15} & \frac{1}{15} & \frac{1}{15} & \frac{1}{15} & \frac{1}{15} & \frac{1}{15} & \frac{1}{15} & \frac{1}{15} \\
\frac{1}{15} & 0 & \frac{1}{140} & \frac{1}{140} & \frac{126}{140} & \frac{1}{140} & \frac{1}{140} & \frac{1}{140} & \frac{1}{140} & \frac{1}{140} & \frac{1}{140} & \frac{1}{140} & \frac{1}{140} & \frac{1}{140} & \frac{1}{140} & \frac{1}{140} \\
\frac{1}{140} & \frac{1}{140} & 0 & \frac{1}{140} & \frac{1}{140} & \frac{1}{140} & \frac{1}{140} & \frac{1}{140} & \frac{126}{140} & \frac{1}{140} & \frac{1}{140} & \frac{1}{140} & \frac{1}{140} & \frac{1}{140} & \frac{1}{140} & \frac{1}{140} \\
\frac{1}{140} & \frac{1}{140} & \frac{1}{140} & 0 & \frac{1}{140} & \frac{1}{140} & \frac{1}{140} & \frac{1}{140} & \frac{1}{140} & \frac{1}{140} & \frac{1}{140} & \frac{1}{140} & \frac{126}{140} & \frac{1}{140} & \frac{1}{140} & \frac{1}{140} \\
\frac{1}{140} & \frac{126}{140} & \frac{1}{140} & \frac{1}{140} & 0 & \frac{1}{140} & \frac{1}{140} & \frac{1}{140} & \frac{1}{140} & \frac{1}{140} & \frac{1}{140} & \frac{1}{140} & \frac{1}{140} & \frac{1}{140} & \frac{1}{140} & \frac{1}{140} \\
\frac{1}{15} & \frac{1}{15} & \frac{1}{15} & \frac{1}{15} & \frac{1}{15} & 0 & \frac{1}{15} & \frac{1}{15} & \frac{1}{15} & \frac{1}{15} & \frac{1}{15} & \frac{1}{15} & \frac{1}{15} & \frac{1}{15} & \frac{1}{15} & \frac{1}{15} \\
\frac{1}{140} & \frac{1}{140} & \frac{1}{140} & \frac{1}{140} & \frac{1}{140} & \frac{1}{140} & 0 & \frac{1}{140} & \frac{1}{140} & \frac{126}{140} & \frac{1}{140} & \frac{1}{140} & \frac{1}{140} & \frac{1}{140} & \frac{1}{140} & \frac{1}{140} \\
\frac{1}{140} & \frac{1}{140} & \frac{1}{140} & \frac{1}{140} & \frac{1}{140} & \frac{1}{140} & \frac{1}{140} & 0 & \frac{1}{140} & \frac{1}{140} & \frac{1}{140} & \frac{1}{140} & \frac{1}{140} & \frac{126}{140} & \frac{1}{140} & \frac{1}{140} \\
\frac{1}{140} & \frac{1}{140} & \frac{126}{140} & \frac{1}{140} & \frac{1}{140} & \frac{1}{140} & \frac{1}{140} & \frac{1}{140} & 0 & \frac{1}{140} & \frac{1}{140} & \frac{1}{140} & \frac{1}{140} & \frac{1}{140} & \frac{1}{140} & \frac{1}{140} \\
\frac{1}{140} & \frac{1}{140} & \frac{1}{140} & \frac{1}{140} & \frac{1}{140} & \frac{1}{140} & \frac{126}{140} & \frac{1}{140} & \frac{1}{140} & 0 & \frac{1}{140} & \frac{1}{140} & \frac{1}{140} & \frac{1}{140} & \frac{1}{140} & \frac{1}{140} \\
\frac{1}{15} & \frac{1}{15} & \frac{1}{15} & \frac{1}{15} & \frac{1}{15} & \frac{1}{15} & \frac{1}{15} & \frac{1}{15} & \frac{1}{15} & \frac{1}{15} & 0 & \frac{1}{15} & \frac{1}{15} & \frac{1}{15} & \frac{1}{15} & \frac{1}{15} \\
\frac{1}{140} & \frac{1}{140} & \frac{1}{140} & \frac{1}{140} & \frac{1}{140} & \frac{1}{140} & \frac{1}{140} & \frac{1}{140} & \frac{1}{140} & \frac{1}{140} & \frac{1}{140} & 0 & \frac{1}{140} & \frac{1}{140} & \frac{126}{140} & \frac{1}{140} \\
\frac{1}{140} & \frac{1}{140} & \frac{1}{140} & \frac{126}{140} & \frac{1}{140} & \frac{1}{140} & \frac{1}{140} & \frac{1}{140} & \frac{1}{140} & \frac{1}{140} & \frac{1}{140} & \frac{1}{140} & 0 & \frac{1}{140} & \frac{1}{140} & \frac{1}{140} \\
\frac{1}{140} & \frac{1}{140} & \frac{1}{140} & \frac{1}{140} & \frac{1}{140} & \frac{1}{140} & \frac{1}{140} & \frac{126}{140} & \frac{1}{140} & \frac{1}{140} & \frac{1}{140} & \frac{1}{140} & \frac{1}{140} & 0 & \frac{1}{140} & \frac{1}{140} \\
\frac{1}{140} & \frac{1}{140} & \frac{1}{140} & \frac{1}{140} & \frac{1}{140} & \frac{1}{140} & \frac{1}{140} & \frac{1}{140} & \frac{1}{140} & \frac{1}{140} & \frac{1}{140} & \frac{126}{140} & \frac{1}{140} & \frac{1}{140} & 0 & \frac{1}{140} \\
\frac{1}{15} & \frac{1}{15} & \frac{1}{15} & \frac{1}{15} & \frac{1}{15} & \frac{1}{15} & \frac{1}{15} & \frac{1}{15} & \frac{1}{15} & \frac{1}{15} & \frac{1}{15} & \frac{1}{15} & \frac{1}{15} & \frac{1}{15} & \frac{1}{15} & 0
\end{bmatrix}
$$

APPENDIX A.4 F_{ij} MATRIX FOR HOTSPOT TRAFFIC

$$f_{ij_{hotspot}} = \begin{bmatrix}
0 & \frac{2}{35} & \frac{2}{35} & \frac{2}{35} & \frac{2}{35} & \frac{2}{35} & \frac{7}{35} & \frac{2}{35} & \frac{2}{35} & \frac{2}{35} & \frac{2}{35} & \frac{2}{35} & \frac{2}{35} & \frac{2}{35} & \frac{2}{35} & \frac{2}{35} \\
\frac{2}{35} & 0 & \frac{2}{35} & \frac{2}{35} & \frac{2}{35} & \frac{2}{35} & \frac{7}{35} & \frac{2}{35} & \frac{2}{35} & \frac{2}{35} & \frac{2}{35} & \frac{2}{35} & \frac{2}{35} & \frac{2}{35} & \frac{2}{35} & \frac{2}{35} \\
\frac{2}{35} & \frac{2}{35} & 0 & \frac{2}{35} & \frac{2}{35} & \frac{2}{35} & \frac{7}{35} & \frac{2}{35} & \frac{2}{35} & \frac{2}{35} & \frac{2}{35} & \frac{2}{35} & \frac{2}{35} & \frac{2}{35} & \frac{2}{35} & \frac{2}{35} \\
\frac{2}{35} & \frac{2}{35} & \frac{2}{35} & 0 & \frac{2}{35} & \frac{2}{35} & \frac{7}{35} & \frac{2}{35} & \frac{2}{35} & \frac{2}{35} & \frac{2}{35} & \frac{2}{35} & \frac{2}{35} & \frac{2}{35} & \frac{2}{35} & \frac{2}{35} \\
\frac{2}{35} & \frac{2}{35} & \frac{2}{35} & \frac{2}{35} & 0 & \frac{2}{35} & \frac{7}{35} & \frac{2}{35} & \frac{2}{35} & \frac{2}{35} & \frac{2}{35} & \frac{2}{35} & \frac{2}{35} & \frac{2}{35} & \frac{2}{35} & \frac{2}{35} \\
\frac{2}{35} & \frac{2}{35} & \frac{2}{35} & \frac{2}{35} & \frac{2}{35} & 0 & \frac{7}{35} & \frac{2}{35} & \frac{2}{35} & \frac{2}{35} & \frac{2}{35} & \frac{2}{35} & \frac{2}{35} & \frac{2}{35} & \frac{2}{35} & \frac{2}{35} \\
\frac{1}{15} & \frac{1}{15} & \frac{1}{15} & \frac{1}{15} & \frac{1}{15} & \frac{1}{15} & 0 & \frac{1}{15} & \frac{1}{15} & \frac{1}{15} & \frac{1}{15} & \frac{1}{15} & \frac{1}{15} & \frac{1}{15} & \frac{1}{15} & \frac{1}{15} \\
\frac{2}{35} & \frac{2}{35} & \frac{2}{35} & \frac{2}{35} & \frac{2}{35} & \frac{2}{35} & \frac{7}{35} & 0 & \frac{2}{35} & \frac{2}{35} & \frac{2}{35} & \frac{2}{35} & \frac{2}{35} & \frac{2}{35} & \frac{2}{35} & \frac{2}{35} \\
\frac{2}{35} & \frac{2}{35} & \frac{2}{35} & \frac{2}{35} & \frac{2}{35} & \frac{2}{35} & \frac{7}{35} & \frac{2}{35} & 0 & \frac{2}{35} & \frac{2}{35} & \frac{2}{35} & \frac{2}{35} & \frac{2}{35} & \frac{2}{35} & \frac{2}{35} \\
\frac{2}{35} & \frac{2}{35} & \frac{2}{35} & \frac{2}{35} & \frac{2}{35} & \frac{2}{35} & \frac{7}{35} & \frac{2}{35} & \frac{2}{35} & 0 & \frac{2}{35} & \frac{2}{35} & \frac{2}{35} & \frac{2}{35} & \frac{2}{35} & \frac{2}{35} \\
\frac{2}{35} & \frac{2}{35} & \frac{2}{35} & \frac{2}{35} & \frac{2}{35} & \frac{2}{35} & \frac{7}{35} & \frac{2}{35} & \frac{2}{35} & \frac{2}{35} & 0 & \frac{2}{35} & \frac{2}{35} & \frac{2}{35} & \frac{2}{35} & \frac{2}{35} \\
\frac{2}{35} & \frac{2}{35} & \frac{2}{35} & \frac{2}{35} & \frac{2}{35} & \frac{2}{35} & \frac{7}{35} & \frac{2}{35} & \frac{2}{35} & \frac{2}{35} & \frac{2}{35} & 0 & \frac{2}{35} & \frac{2}{35} & \frac{2}{35} & \frac{2}{35} \\
\frac{2}{35} & \frac{2}{35} & \frac{2}{35} & \frac{2}{35} & \frac{2}{35} & \frac{2}{35} & \frac{7}{35} & \frac{2}{35} & \frac{2}{35} & \frac{2}{35} & \frac{2}{35} & \frac{2}{35} & 0 & \frac{2}{35} & \frac{2}{35} & \frac{2}{35} \\
\frac{2}{35} & \frac{2}{35} & \frac{2}{35} & \frac{2}{35} & \frac{2}{35} & \frac{2}{35} & \frac{7}{35} & \frac{2}{35} & \frac{2}{35} & \frac{2}{35} & \frac{2}{35} & \frac{2}{35} & \frac{2}{35} & 0 & \frac{2}{35} & \frac{2}{35} \\
\frac{2}{35} & \frac{2}{35} & \frac{2}{35} & \frac{2}{35} & \frac{2}{35} & \frac{2}{35} & \frac{7}{35} & \frac{2}{35} & \frac{2}{35} & \frac{2}{35} & \frac{2}{35} & \frac{2}{35} & \frac{2}{35} & \frac{2}{35} & 0 & \frac{2}{35} \\
\frac{2}{35} & \frac{2}{35} & \frac{2}{35} & \frac{2}{35} & \frac{2}{35} & \frac{2}{35} & \frac{7}{35} & \frac{2}{35} & \frac{2}{35} & \frac{2}{35} & \frac{2}{35} & \frac{2}{35} & \frac{2}{35} & \frac{2}{35} & \frac{2}{35} & 0
\end{bmatrix}$$

CHAPTER 4

Wireless Small-World NoCs

According to the International Technology Roadmap for Semiconductors (ITRS), interconnects are the major bottlenecks to overcoming the power-performance barrier for future technology generations. With shrinking geometry, the interwire spacing decreases rapidly (Ho et al., 2001) while the height and width of the wires does not scale at the same rate. This, in turn, tends to increase the cross-sectional aspect ratio, increasing the effective coupling capacitance between intralayer adjacent wires with negative effects on delay, power, and signal integrity. This clearly indicates the challenges facing future chip designers associated with traditional scaling of conventional on-chip, metal-/dielectric-based interconnects. To enhance the performance of such conventional interconnect-based multicore chips, wireless technologies need to be employed. These wireless technologies, along with appropriate signaling techniques, have been predicted to be capable of enabling larger multicore Network-on-Chip (NoC) designs, which improves the speed and energy dissipation in data transfer significantly.

WIRELESS PHYSICAL LAYER DESIGN

Millimeter-Wave Antennas

One option for wireless NoC antennas are millimeter-wave (mm-wave) antennas. The performance of silicon-integrated mm-wave on-chip antennas for intra- and interchip communication with longer range have been already demonstrated by the authors of Lin et al. (2007). They have primarily used metal zigzag antennas operating in the range of tens of GHz. The propagation mechanisms of radiowaves over intrachip channels with integrated antennas were also investigated (Zhang et al., 2007). It was shown that zigzag monopole antennas of axial length 1−2 mm can achieve a communication range of about 10−15 mm. Depending on the antenna configuration and substrate characteristics, the achievable frequency of the wireless channel can be in the range of 50−100 GHz. The design of a hierarchical wireless NoC with mm-wave wireless links is proposed in Deb et al. (2010). In

Lee et al. (2009), the feasibility of designing miniature on-chip antennas and simple transceivers that operate at 100–500 GHz range has been demonstrated. The on-chip antenna in Lee et al. (2009) is placed in a polyimide layer to reduce the substrate loss. Using this configuration, the range of communication has been extended to 1 cm. A relatively long intrachip communication range facilitates single-hop communication between widely separated blocks. This is essential to achieve the full benefit of on-chip wireless networks for multicore systems by reducing long distance multihop wireline communication.

For a mm-wave wireless NoC, the two principal wireless interface (WI) components are the antenna and the transceiver. A metal zigzag antenna has been demonstrated to possess the best power gain for the smallest area (Floyd et al., 2002). This antenna also has negligible effect of rotation (relative angle between transmitting and receiving antennas) on received signal strength. Zigzag antenna characteristics depend on physical parameters like axial length, trace width, arm length, bend angle, etc. By varying these parameters, the antennas are designed to operate on different frequency channels (Deb et al., 2013). The antenna design ensures that signals outside the communication bandwidth, for each channel, are sufficiently attenuated to avoid interchannel interference.

The design of a low-power wideband wireless transceiver is the key to guarantee the desired performance. Therefore, at both the architecture and circuit levels of the transceiver, low-power design considerations need to be taken into account. At the architecture level, on-off-keying (OOK) modulation can be chosen. OOK modulation is a good choice as it simplifies circuit design, has small area overhead for circuit implementation, as well as being relatively power efficient. Noncoherent demodulation is used, therefore eliminating the power-hungry phase-lock loop in the transceiver. Moreover, at the circuit level, body-enabled design techniques (Yu et al., 2011), including both forward body bias with DC voltages, as well as body-driven by AC signals, can be implemented in several subblocks to further decrease their power consumption.

The transceiver architecture is shown in Fig. 4.1. The receiver (RX) includes a wideband low-noise amplifier (LNA), an envelope detector for noncoherent demodulation, and a baseband amplifier. A local oscillator is not needed in the RX because noncoherent demodulation is used which results in a power reduction by more than 30% compared to the proposed transceiver of Deb et al. (2013).

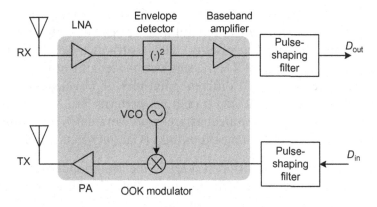

Figure 4.1 Block diagram of the noncoherent OOK transceiver for a mm-wave small-world NoC.

The transmitter (TX) has a simple direct up-conversion topology, consisting of a body-driven OOK modulator, a wideband power amplifier (PA), and a voltage-controlled oscillator (VCO).

Carbon Nanotube Antennas

Another option being explored for wireless NoCs is to use carbon nanotube (CNT) antennas, which can outperform conventional wireline counterparts significantly (Ganguly et al., 2011). Antenna characteristics of CNTs, in the THz frequency range, have been investigated both theoretically and experimentally (Kempa et al., 2007). Bundles of CNTs are predicted to enhance performance of antenna modules by up to 40 dB in radiation efficiency and provide excellent directional properties in far-field patterns (Shacham et al., 2008). Moreover, these antennas can achieve a bandwidth of around 500 GHz, whereas the antennas operating in the mm-wave range achieve bandwidths of 10s of GHz. Thus antennas operating in the THz/optical frequency range can support much higher data rates. CNTs have numerous characteristics that make them suitable as on-chip antenna elements for optical frequencies. Given wavelengths of hundreds of nanometers to several micrometers, there is a need for virtually one-dimensional antenna structures for efficient transmission and reception. With diameters of a few nanometers and any length up to a few millimeters possible, CNTs are the perfect candidate. Such thin structures are almost impossible to achieve with traditional micro-fabrication techniques for metals. Virtually defect-free CNT structures do not suffer from power loss due to surface roughness and edge imperfections found in traditional metallic antennas.

Radiation characteristics of multiwalled CNT (MWCNT) antennas are observed to be in excellent quantitative agreement with traditional radio antenna theory (Kempa et al., 2007), although at much higher frequencies of hundreds of THz. Using various lengths of the antenna elements, corresponding to different multiples of wavelengths of the external lasers, scattering and radiation patterns are shown to be improved. Such nanotube antennas are good candidates for establishing on-chip wireless communications links (Ganguly et al., 2011).

Chemical vapor deposition (CVD) is the traditional method for growing nanotubes in specific locations by using lithographically patterned catalyst islands. The application of an electric field during growth, or the direction of gas flow, during CVD can help align the nanotubes. As high-temperature CVD has a high chance of damaging the preexisting CMOS layers it suffers from successful integration leading to a higher percentage of defects on the silicon. To help alleviate the issues of damaging the preexisting CMOS layers, localized heaters in the CMOS fabrication process can enable localized CVD of nanotubes without exposing the entire chip to high temperatures, used in Zhou et al. (2008); however, the silicon directly below the localized heaters can still be damaged.

COMMUNICATION AND CHANNELIZATION

Millimeter-Wave Communication

In an NoC that uses mm-wave antennas, data is generally transferred via a flit-based, wormhole routing (Pande et al., 2005). Between a source–destination pair, the wireless links, through the WIs, are only chosen if the wireless path reduces the total path length compared to the wireline path. This can potentially give rise to hotspot situations in the WIs. Many messages will try to access the wireless shortcuts simultaneously, thus overloading the WIs, which would result in higher latency and energy dissipation. Token flow control (Kumar et al., 2008) is used to alleviate overloading at the WIs. An arbitration mechanism is designed to grant access to the wireless medium to a particular WI, including the gateway WI (a special WI that operates on all the wireless frequency channels used in the network), at a given instant to avoid interference and contention between the WIs that have the same frequency. To avoid the need for centralized control and synchronization, the arbitration policy adopted is a wireless token passing protocol (Deb et al., 2013). In this scheme, a single flit circulates as a token in each frequency channel. The particular WIs possessing the wireless token is allowed to broadcast flits into the wireless medium, for the wireless token's respective frequency. The wireless token is forwarded to the next WI, operating in the same frequency channel, after all flits belonging to a message at a particular WI are transmitted. Packets are rerouted, through an alternate wireline path, if the WI buffers are full or, it does not have the token.

CNT Communication

By using multiband laser sources to excite the CNT antennas, different frequency channels can be assigned to pairs of communicating source and destination nodes. This will require using antenna elements tuned to different frequencies for each pair, thus creating a form of frequency division multiplexing, giving rise to dedicated channels between source and destination pairs. This is possible by using CNTs of different lengths, which are multiples of the wavelengths of the respective carrier frequencies. High directional gains of these antennas, demonstrated in Kempa et al. (2007), aid in creating directed channels between source and destination pairs. In Lee et al. (2009), 24 continuous wave laser sources of different frequencies are used. Thus, these 24 different frequencies can be assigned to multiple wireless links in the NoC architecture in such a way that a single frequency channel is used only once to avoid signal interference on the same frequencies. This enables concurrent use of multiband channels over the chip; hence, 24 wireless links each with a single channel. The laser sources can be located off-chip or bonded to the silicon die (Shacham et al., 2008). Currently, high-speed silicon-integrated Mach−Zehnder optical modulators and demodulators, which convert electrical signals to optical signals and vice versa are commercially available (Green et al., 2007). The optical modulators can provide 10 Gbps data rate per channel on these links. At the receiver, an LNA can be used to boost the power of the received electrical signal, which will then be routed to the destination switch. The modulation scheme adopted is noncoherent, OOK, and therefore does not require complex clock recovery and synchronization circuits. The main reason for choosing OOK modulation is due to the small area overhead to implement the modulation scheme. Due to limitations in the number of distinct frequency channels that can be created through the CNT antennas, the flit width in NoCs is generally higher than the number of possible channels per link. Also, the flit width is smaller than the capacity of a single link. Thus, to send a whole flit through the wireless link, using a single channel, while also utilizing the full capacity of the link, a proper channelization scheme needs to be adopted. Therefore, time division multiplexing is adopted (Ganguly et al., 2011). The various components of the THz wireless transceiver, viz., the electrooptic modulators, the TDM modulator/demodulator, and the LNA are implemented as a whole part known as a wireless port (WP) that is connected to an NoC switch where the wireless channel is to be implemented.

TOPOLOGY OF WIRELESS NoCs

Topology of CNT and mm-Wave SWNoC

As long-wired interconnects are extremely costly both in terms of energy and latency, wireless links can be established to connect switches that are separated by a long distance. Depending upon the available wireless resources, there is a constraint on the maximum number of possible wireless links in the small-world NoC. It has many short-range local links from the SW network creation, as well as a few long-range shortcuts that will be made into wireless links.

In the CNT SWNoC (CSWNoC) and the mm-wave SWNoC (mSWNoC) topologies, each core is connected to a switch and the switches are interconnected using both wireline and wireless links. The topology of the SWNoCs are a small-world network where the links between switches are established following a power-law model (Petermann and De Los Rios, 2005; Wettin et al., 2013). In these small-world networks there are still several long wireline interconnects. As these are extremely costly in terms of power and delay, we use either CNT or mm-wave wireless links to connect switches that are separated by a long distance. In Deb et al. (2013), it is demonstrated that it is possible to create three nonoverlapping channels with on-chip mm-wave wireless links. Using these three channels, we overlay the wireline small-world connectivity with the wireless links such that a few switches get an additional WP. Each of these WPs will have WIs tuned to one of the three different frequency channels. Each WI in the network is then assigned one of the three channels; more frequently communicating WIs are assigned the same channel to optimize the overall hop-count. One WI is replaced by a gateway WI that has all three channels assigned to it; this facilitates data exchange between the nonoverlapping wireless channels. For CSWNoC, up to 24 wireless links can replace the longest 24 wireline links. Figs. 4.2 and 4.3 show examples of CSWNoC and mSWNoC networks.

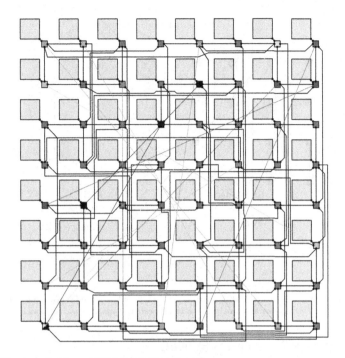

Figure 4.2 Topology of a 64-core CSWNoC with 12 wireless links.

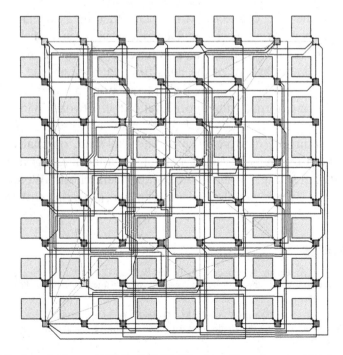

Figure 4.3 Topology of a 64-core mSWNoC with 12 WIs (5th column, 4th row from upper left is the gateway).

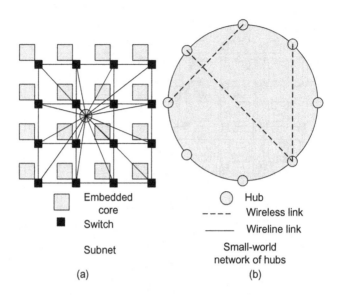

Figure 4.4 Topology of a hierarchical SWNoC (a) subnets and (b) hubs where all switches in a subnet are connected to the hub and the hubs are interconnected by a small-world graph with both wired and wireless links.

Topology of a Hierarchical SWNoC

The architecture of the hierarchical SWNoC is a wireless hybrid-NoC. The whole NoC is subdivided into smaller subnetworks (subnets). Cores within a subnet are connected with each other in a regular wireline network like a mesh, ring, or star. Depending on the size of the subnet, the cores in each subnet are also connected to one or more hubs, through wireline links. All of the hubs from each subnet are then connected among themselves using wireline links, using another regular network, like a ring, forming the upper level of the network. Wireless links are then added to the upper level of the network to create long-range shortcuts within the network. The wireless links are optimally distributed, between the hubs based on a simulated annealing based heuristic (Deb et al., 2013). Fig. 4.4 shows an example hierarchical SWNoC where each subnet is a mesh, and the upper level network is a ring structure.

REFERENCES

Deb, S., Ganguly, A., Chang, K., Pande, P.P., Belzer, B., Heo, D., 2010. Enhancing performance of network-on-chip architectures with millimeter-wave wireless interconnects. In: Proceedings of ASAP, pp. 73–80.

Deb, S., Chang, K., Yu, X., Sah, S., Cosic, M., Ganguly, A., et al., 2013. Design of an energy efficient CMOS compatible NoC architecture with millimeter-wave wireless interconnects. IEEE Trans. Comput. 62 (12), 2382–2396.

Floyd, B.A., Hung, C.-M., O, K.K., 2002. Intra-chip wireless interconnect for clock distribution implemented with integrated antennas, receivers, and transmitters. IEEE J. Solid-State Circuits 37 (5), 543–552.

Ganguly, A., Chang, K., Deb, S., Pande, P.P., Belzer, B., Teuscher, C., 2011. Scalable hybrid wireless network-on-chip architectures for multi-core systems. IEEE Trans. Comput. 60 (10), 1485–1502.

Green, W.M., Rooks, M.J., Sekaric, L., Vlasov, Y.A., 2007. Ultra-compact, low RF power, 10 Gb/s silicon Mach-Zehnder modulator. Opt. Express 15 (25), 17106–17113.

Ho, R., Mai, K.W., Horowitz, M.A., 2001. The future of wires. Proc. IEEE 89 (4), 490–504.

Kempa, K., Rybczynski, J., Huang, Z., Gregorczyk, K., Vidan, A., Kimball, B., et al., 2007. Carbon nanotubes as optical antennae. Adv. Mater. 19 (3), 421–426.

Kumar, A., Peh, L.-S., Jha, N.K., 2008. Token flow control. In: Proceedings of MICRO. pp. 342–353.

Lee, S.-B., Tam, S.-W., Pefkianakis, I., Lu, S., Chang, M.F., Guo, C., et al., 2009. A scalable micro wireless interconnect structure for CMPs. In: Proceedings of MobiCom. pp. 20–25.

Lin, J., Wu, H.-T., Su, Y., Gao, L., Sugavanam, A., Brewer, J.E., et al., 2007. Communication using antennas fabricated in silicon integrated circuits. IEEE J. Solid-State Circuits 42 (8), 1678–1687.

Pande, P.P., Grecu, C.S., Jones, M., Ivanov, A., Saleh, R.A., 2005. Performance evaluation and design trade-offs for network-on-chip interconnect architectures. IEEE Trans. Comput. 54 (8), 1025–1040.

Petermann, T., De Los Rios, P., 2005. Spatial small-world networks: a wiring cost perspective. arXiv:cond-mat/0501420v2.

Shacham, A., Bergman, K., Carloni, L.P., 2008. Photonic networks-on-chip for future generations of chip multiprocessors. IEEE Trans. Comput. 57 (9), 1246–1260.

Wettin, P., Murray, J., Pande, P.P., Shirazi, B., Ganguly, A., 2013. Energy-efficient multicore chip design through cross-layer approach. In: Proceedings of DATE, pp. 725–730.

Yu, X., Sah, S.P., Deb, S., Pande, P.P., Belzer, B., Heo, D., 2011. A wideband body-enabled millimeter-wave transceiver for wireless network-on-chip. In: Proceedings of MWSCAS, pp. 1–4.

Zhang, Y.P., Chen, Z.M., Sun, M., 2007. Propagation mechanisms of radio waves over intra-chip channels with integrated antennas: frequency-domain measurements and time-domain analysis. IEEE Trans. Antennas Propag. 55 (10), 2900–2906.

Zhou, Y., Johnson, J.L., Wu, L., Maley, S.B., Ural, A., Xie, H.K., 2008. Design and fabrication of microheaters for localized carbon nanotube growth. In: Proceedings of NANO, pp. 452–455.

CHAPTER 5

Topology-Agnostic Routing for Irregular Networks

As small-world networks are irregular in nature, suitable routing algorithms need to be employed to handle being topology-agnostic and have deadlock freedom. There are two main broad topic routing strategies for irregular networks: rule-driven and path-driven. As the rule- and path-based routing strategies are fundamentally opposite, the design trade-offs need to be determined. Traditionally, these routing strategies have been studied for traditional parallel computing systems where the comparative performance evaluation has been in terms of saturation throughput; however, NoC chip multiprocessor benchmarks can operate far below network saturation. When this occurs, the traffic interaction and density need to be taken into account, as well as the complexity of the routing strategy. Additionally, there has been significant research done toward topology-agnostic routing strategies, some of which were discussed in Chapter 2. In the following chapters, several strategies are explored and expanded to show the capabilities of the wireless SWNoC architectures discussed; however, the architecture is not bound to these specific routing strategies.

A SIMPLE APPROACH TO TOPOLOGY-AGNOSTIC ROUTING

For many irregular NoCs, data is transferred via flit-based, wormhole routing (Deb et al., 2013). To ensure a deadlock-free routing, the Tree-based Routing Architecture for Irregular Networks (TRAIN) algorithm is adopted (Floyd et al., 2002). The TRAIN algorithm is a rule-based routing strategy where the irregular network is turned into a tree-type network. A Minimum Spanning Tree (MST) of the network is created with a randomly selected node as the root. Data can then be routed along the MST with simple rules. After the MST is created, the other links that were not originally included in the MST are (re) introduced as shortcuts within the tree-based network to keep the small-world characteristics of the network intact.

The MST is created with the link lengths as edge weights. The MST minimizes the total edge weight and hence minimizes the average distance between the cores along the tree. The TRAIN algorithm routes all traffic up the tree toward the root until a common branch point is found. When the traffic reaches the common branching point within the tree, the data then follows the branch until it reaches the destination. An allowed route never uses a link in the up direction along the tree after it has been in the down path once. Hence, channel dependency cycles are prohibited, and deadlock freedom is achieved. The shortcuts are used for packet transmission only if they provide a shorter path to the destination than the route along the MST while flits are routed upward along a branch. Livelock is avoided because each packet has a fixed path from its source to destination. The described routing algorithm is elaborated in Fig. 5.1.

ROUTING STRATEGY FOR HIERARCHICAL WIRELESS SMALL-WORLD NETWORKS

For hierarchical SWNoCs, intrasubnet data routing is done according to the topology of the subnets. If the subnet is mesh-based, then routing can be done with dimension order or e-cube routing. If the subnet is tree-based, then routing can be done with an up/down routing strategy. The exact strategy does not matter besides being deadlock free which is a requirement. Inter-subnet data routing, however, requires the flits to use the upper level network consisting of both wired and wireless links. Again, the exact routing for the upper level does not matter as long as the deadlock free requirement is met. If the upper level of the network resembles a tree or truly is irregular, then the TRAIN algorithm mentioned above would be a good choice. If the upper level of the network resembles a mesh like structure with wireless shortcuts, then the south-east type routing strategy would be the best choice. If the source hub in the upper level of the network does not have a wireless link, the flits are routed to the nearest hub with a wireless link via the wired links and are transmitted through the wireless channel. Likewise, if the destination hub does not have a wireless link, then the hub nearest to it with a wireless link receives the data and routes it to the destination through wired links. Between a pair of source and destination hubs without wireless links, the routing path involving a wireless link is chosen if it reduces the total path length compared to the completely wired path.

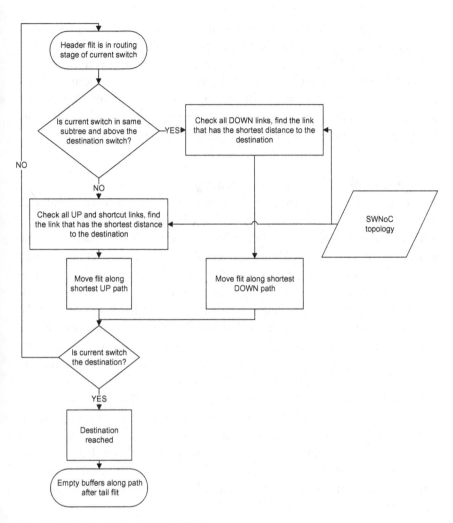

Figure 5.1 TRAIN routing flowchart for SWNoC.

ADVANCED ROUTING STRATEGIES FOR WIRELESS SMALL-WORLD NETWORKS

Two different types of routing strategies were developed for mm-wave wireless SWNoCs: a rule-based and path-based routing strategy. In the rule-based routing, a spanning tree of the network is created where data is routed along the spanning tree, similar to the TRAIN algorithm mentioned earlier in this chapter. An allowed route never uses a link in the up direction along the tree after it has been in the down direction once. Hence, channel dependency cycles are prohibited, and deadlock freedom is achieved (Chi and Tang, 1997). However, a well-known weakness of this routing scheme is that it has a strong tendency to generate hotspots around the root of the tree structure. In the path-based routing, the network resources are divided into layers and network deadlocks are avoided by preventing portions of traffic from using specific layers (Flich et al., 2012; Lysne et al., 2006).

Rule-Based MROOTS Routing Strategy
The first routing strategy that we consider is an up/down tree-based routing algorithm, belonging to the rule-based classification, for the SWNoC that utilizes a multiple tree roots (MROOTS)-based mechanism (Chi and Tang, 1997; Flich et al., 2012; Lysne et al., 2006). MROOTS allows multiple routing trees to exist, where each tree routes on a dedicated virtual channel. Hence, traffic bottlenecks can be reduced in the upper tree levels that are inherent in this type of routing. Breadth-first trees were used during the tree creation process to balance the traffic distribution among the subtrees and to minimize bottlenecks in a particular tree. All wireless and wireline links that are not part of the breadth-first tree are reintroduced as shortcuts. An allowed route never uses an up direction along the tree after it has been in the down path once. In addition, a packet traveling in the downward direction is not allowed to take a shortcut, even if that minimizes the distance to the destination. Hence, channel dependency cycles are prohibited, and deadlock freedom is achieved (Chi and Tang, 1997). A flowchart of the adopted MROOTS routing strategy is shown in Fig. 5.2.

For the different breadth-first trees, multiple tree root selection policies can be adopted, viz., a random root placement (random), a maximized intraroot tree distance placement (max distance), and a traffic-weighted minimized hop-count placement (f_{ij}). The random root placement chooses the roots at random locations within the network. The maximized intraroot tree distance placement attempts to find roots that are far apart in the tree (Lysne et al., 2006), in order to minimize the congestion near the selected roots. Finally, the traffic-weighted minimized hop-count placement is described as follows. Selecting M tree roots will create M trees in the network, where the chosen M roots minimize the optimization metric μ as defined in (5.1).

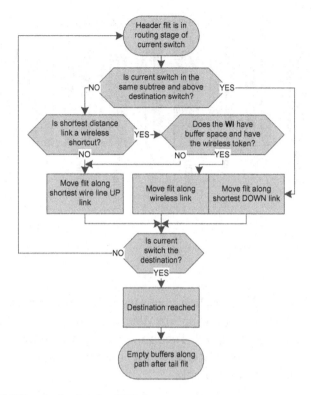

Figure 5.2 MROOTS routing flowchart for mSWNoC.

$$\mu = \min_{\forall \text{ roots}} \sum_{\forall i} \sum_{\forall j} h_{ij} f_{ij} \qquad (5.1)$$

Here, the minimum path distance in hops, h_{ij}, from switch i to switch j is determined following the up/down routing restrictions. The frequency of traffic interaction between the switches is denoted by f_{ij}. As root selection only affects valid routing paths for deadlock freedom and does not alter the physical placement of links, any a priori knowledge of the frequency of traffic interaction aids in root selection. Incorporating f_{ij} helps minimize the routed path lengths for specific workloads on the SWNoC architecture.

Fig. 5.3 shows the variation of the energy–delay product with respect to the location of the roots for MROOTS using various benchmarks. It can be seen in Fig. 5.3 that the traffic-weighted minimized hop-count (f_{ij}) obtains the minimum energy–delay product. This is

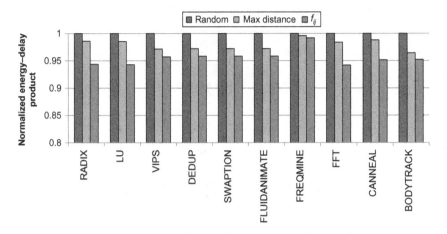

Figure 5.3 Normalized energy–delay product for mSWNoC with different root placement strategies for MROOTS.

due to the fact that the highest communicating switches are placed at the roots, effectively allowing for the shortest path routing to be employed for these switches. Therefore, the f_{ij} root selection strategy will be employed for MROOTS for the performance evaluations throughout the rest of this book.

Path-Based ALASH Routing Strategy

The second routing strategy is an adaptive layered shortest path (ALASH) routing algorithm (Lysne et al., 2006), which belongs to the path-based classification. ALASH is built upon the layered shortest path (LASH) algorithm, but has more flexibility by allowing each message to adaptively switch paths, letting the message choose its own route at every intermediate switch.

The LASH algorithm takes advantage of the multiple virtual channels in each switch port of the NoC switches in order to route messages along the shortest physical paths. In order to achieve deadlock freedom, the network is divided into a set of virtual layers, which are created by dedicating the virtual channels from each switch port into these layers. The shortest physical path between each source–destination pair is then assigned to a layer such that the layer's channel dependency graph remains free from cycles. A channel dependency is created between two links in the source–destination path when a link from switch i to switch j and a link from switch j to switch

k satisfies the following condition, *pathlength(i)* < *pathlength(j)* < *pathlength(k)*, where *pathlength(X)* is the length of the minimal path between switch X and the original source switch. When a layer's channel dependency graph has no cycles, it is free from deadlocks as elaborated in Lysne et al. (2006).

For ALASH, the decision to switch paths is based on the current network conditions. Virtual channel availability and current communication density of the network are used as the two relevant parameters for this purpose. The communication density is defined as the number of flits traversing the given switch or link over a certain time interval. In order to increase the adaptability of the routing, multiple shortest paths between all source–destination pairs are found and then included into as many layers as possible. The message route through the network depends on the layers each source–destination pair use. Therefore, the layering function that controls how the layers are allocated for each source–destination pair has an impact on the latency and energy profile of the NoC.

Randomized uniform layering function (random), a layer balancing function (virtual), and a priority-based layering function (priority) are three different examples of layering functions that can be used for ALASH. The uniform layering function selects source–destination pairs at random while allocating layers to them, giving each source–destination pair an equal opportunity for each layer; unless including the path results in a cyclic dependency. The virtual layering function uses the apriori knowledge of the frequency of traffic interactions, f_{ij}, in order to evenly distribute source–destination pairs with large f_{ij} values across the different layers. In contrary, the priority layering function allocates as many layers as possible to source–destination pairs with high f_{ij}. This improves the adaptability of messages with higher f_{ij} by providing the messages with greater routing flexibility. As an example, Fig. 5.4 shows the priority layering function flowchart.

The main goal of these different layering functions is to help distribute the messages across the network in such a way so as not to induce a load imbalance in any layer and hence, any particular network switch. The virtual layering function does this by reducing the opportunity that source–destination pairs with high f_{ij} values will use the same layer. The priority layering function does the same by allowing the source–destination pairs with high f_{ij} values to get more layers to use

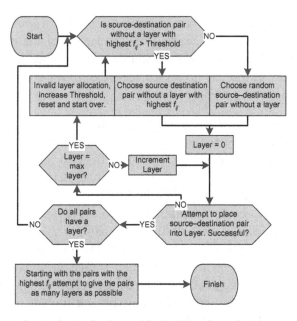

Figure 5.4 The priority layering function flowchart used for ALASH to allocate the layers.

adaptively. This avoids use of the same layer by another source–destination pair with high f_{ij} values. For every layer balancing technique, it is possible to induce deadlocks if a message is allowed to switch back and forth between two or more layers. Hence, a message is not allowed to revisit a layer that it has previously traveled in to maintain deadlock freedom. A flowchart of the adopted ALASH routing strategy is shown in Fig. 5.5

Fig. 5.6 shows the variation of the energy–delay product with respect to the priority layering function for ALASH using various benchmarks. It can be seen in Fig. 5.6 that the priority layering function (priority) obtains the minimum energy–delay product. This is due to the fact that the highest communicating source–destination pairs are given the most resources, allowing the adaptability in ALASH to work at its best.

Fig. 5.7 shows the normalized flits per link distribution in the network for the CANNEAL benchmark. It can be seen from Fig. 5.7 that for both layering functions, the minimum, the first quartile, and median are the same values; while the values for the third quartile are very similar. This indicates that the traffic distribution for both

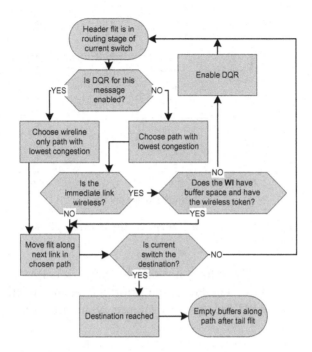

Figure 5.5 ALASH routing flowchart for mSWNoC.

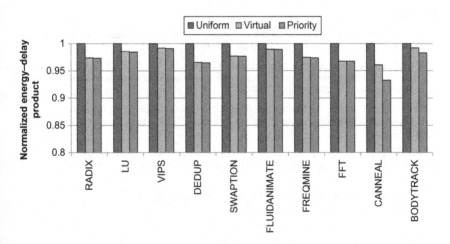

Figure 5.6 Normalized energy–delay product for mSWNoC with different layering strategies for ALASH.

layering functions is similar. We should then focus on the flits per link for the highly utilized links. Fig. 5.7 shows that the flit traversal for these links (indicated by the maximum) is lowered for the priority layering function. This shows that the priority layering function routes

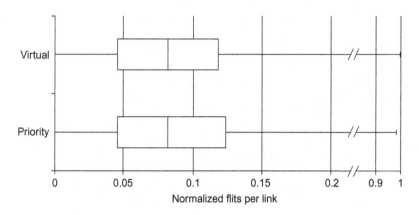

Figure 5.7 Normalized flits per link distribution for the two different layering functions of ALASH for the CANNEAL benchmark.

flits away from heavily utilized links in the network better than the virtual layering function. Therefore, the priority layering function will be employed for ALASH for the performance evaluations throughout the rest of this book.

REFERENCES

Chi, H.-C., Tang, C.-T., 1997. A deadlock-free routing scheme for interconnection networks with irregular topology. In: Proceedings of ICPADS, pp. 88–95.

Deb, S., Chang, K., Yu, X., Sah, S., Cosic, M., Ganguly, A., et al., 2013. Design of an energy efficient CMOS compatible NoC architecture with millimeter-wave wireless interconnects. IEEE Trans. Comput. 62 (12), 2382–2396.

Flich, J., Skeie, T., Mejía, A., Lysne, O., López, P., Robles, A., et al., 2012. A survey and evaluation of topology-agnostic deterministic routing algorithms. IEEE Trans. Parallel Distrib. Syst. 23 (3), 405–425.

Floyd, B.A., Hung, C.-M., O, K.K., 2002. Intra-chip wireless interconnect for clock distribution implemented with integrated antennas, receivers, and transmitters. IEEE J. Solid-State Circuits 37 (5), 543–552.

Lysne, O., Skeie, T., Reinemo, S.-A., Theiss, I., 2006. Layered routing in irregular networks. IEEE Trans. Parallel Distrib. Syst. 17 (1), 51–65.

CHAPTER 6

Performance Evaluation and Design Trade-Offs of Wireless SWNoCs

In this chapter the performance of CSWNoC and mSWNoC are characterized against a conventional wireline mesh-based NoC. The architectures considered in this chapter are evaluated using a cycle accurate simulator in conjunction with GEM5 (gem5.org) (Binkert et al., 2011) to obtain detailed processor- and network-level information. We consider a system of 64 alpha cores running Linux within the GEM5 platform for all experiments. Three SPLASH-2 benchmarks, FFT, RADIX, LU (Woo et al., 1995), and seven PARSEC benchmarks, CANNEAL, BODYTRACK, VIPS, DEDUP, SWAPTION, FLUIDANIMATE, and FREQMINE (Bienia, 2011) as well as three synthetic benchmarks, uniform random, transpose, and hotspot are considered. The synthetic benchmarks allow for exploration of larger system sizes which are included in this chapter. The GEM5 platform has a core limitation of 64 cores for full-system simulations which is how traces were gathered for the SPLASH-2 and PARSEC benchmarks. These benchmarks vary in characteristics from computation intensive to communication intensive in nature and thus are of particular interest in this work. The interswitch traffic patterns in terms of normalized switch interaction rates for the SPLASH-2 and PARSEC benchmarks are shown in Fig. 6.1 using a system of 64 alpha cores running Linux within the GEM5 platform, where each benchmark is running 64 threads. The benchmarks that are communication intensive, CANNEAL and BODYTRACK, have higher switch interaction rates than the others. It can be seen in Fig. 6.1 that the medians of the interaction rate for these two benchmarks are higher than the medians of the other benchmarks. The median switch interaction rates of the other benchmarks are low, but are not exactly the same. As an example, FFT has a relatively high median switch interaction rate when compared to the other computation-intensive benchmarks, but when compared to the communication-intensive benchmarks, it is an order of magnitude lower. The switch interaction rate of these benchmarks plays an

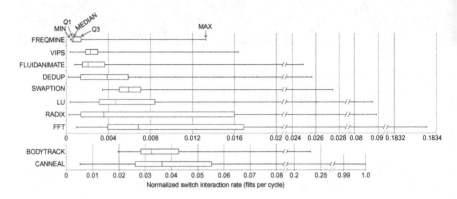

Figure 6.1 Normalized switch interaction rates for the SPLASH-2 benchmarks: FFT, RADIX, and LU and the PARSEC benchmarks: FREQMINE, VIPS, LUIDANIMATE, DEDUP, SWAPTION, BODYTRACK, and CANNEAL.

important role in the overall latency, energy dissipation, and thermal profiles of the small-world NoC (SWNoC), as explained later. $Q1$ and $Q3$ in Fig. 6.1 stand for the first and third quartiles, respectively.

The NoC switches have three functional stages: input arbitration, routing/switch traversal, and output arbitration (Dally and Towles, 2001). The input and output ports, including the WPs, have four virtual channels per port, each having a buffer depth of 2 flits. Each packet consists of 64 flits. Similar to the wired links, we have adopted wormhole routing in the wireless links also. A simple flow control mechanism is adopted uniformly for wireless links in which the sender WP stops transmitting flits only when a full signal is asserted from the receiver WP. This full signal is embedded in a control flit sent from the receiver to the sender only when the receiver buffer is filled above a predefined threshold.

The network switches are synthesized from an RTL level design using 65 nm standard cell libraries from CMP (http://cmp.imag.fr), using Synopsys Design Vision. The NoC switches are driven with a clock of frequency 2.5 GHz. The delays and energy dissipation on the wired links were obtained through Cadence layout and taking into account the specific lengths of each link based on the established connections in the 20-mm × 20-mm die following the logical connectivity of the small-world topology.

The bandwidth of the millimeter (mm)-wave and carbon nanotube (CNT) wireless links is considered to be 16 and 10 Gbps per channel, respectively. The energy dissipations of the mm-wave and CNT wireless links were obtained through analytical and experimental findings as shown in Chang et al. (2012) and Ganguly et al. (2009). Considering the energy dissipation of the transmitting and receiving antennas, and all the necessary components of the transmitter and receiver circuitry, the energy dissipation of the longest CNT wireless link of 23 mm sustaining a data rate of 10 Gbps on the chip is 0.33 pJ/bit (Ganguly et al., 2009) and the longest mm-wave wireless link of 20 mm sustaining a data rate of 16 Gpbs on the chip is 2.3 pJ/bit (Chang et al., 2012), both of which are significantly less than even the most efficient conventional metal wires. The energy dissipation of the NoC switches is obtained by feeding a large set of data patterns into the gate-level netlist and by running Synopsys Prime Power.

All ports except those associated with the WIs, as explained in Chapter 4 have a buffer depth of two flits and each switch port has four virtual channels. Hence, four trees and four layers are created in MROOTS and ALASH, respectively. The ports associated with the WIs have an increased buffer depth of eight flits to avoid excessive latency penalties while waiting for the token. Increasing the buffer depth beyond this limit does not produce any further performance improvement for this particular packet size, but will give rise to additional area overhead (Deb et al., 2013). Energy dissipation of the network switches, inclusive of the routing strategies, were obtained from the synthesized netlist by running Synopsys Prime Power, while the energy dissipated by wireline links was obtained through HSPICE simulations, taking into consideration the length of the wireline links. The processor-level statistics generated by the GEM5 simulations are incorporated into McPAT (Multicore Power, Area, and Timing) to determine the processor-level power values (Li et al., 2009).

After obtaining the processor and network power values, these elements are arranged on a 20-mm × 20-mm die. The floor plans, along with the power values, are used in HotSpot (Skadron et al., 2003) to obtain steady-state thermal profiles. The processor power and the architecture-dependent network power values in the presence of the specific benchmarks are fed to the HotSpot simulator to obtain their temperature profiles.

PERFORMANCE METRICS

To characterize the performance of the proposed CSWNoC and mSWNoC architectures, we consider two network parameters: throughput and energy dissipation. Throughput is defined as the average number of flits successfully received per embedded core per clock cycle. The throughput, t, is calculated according to

$$t = \frac{\mu_C \varphi}{N T_{\text{sim}}} \tag{6.1}$$

where μ_C is the total number of messages successfully routed, φ is the size of a single message in number of flits, N is the total number of cores in the NoC, and T_{sim} is the simulation duration in number of cycles.

As a measurement of energy, we use the average energy dissipation per packet. Energy dissipation per packet is the average energy dissipated by a single packet when routed from the source to the destination node through multiple switches, wired, and wireless links. For the wireless links, the main contribution to energy dissipation comes from the WPs, which include antennas, transceiver circuits, and other communication modules like the TDM block and the LNA. Energy dissipation per packet, E_{pkt}, can be calculated according to

$$E_{\text{pkt}} = \frac{\sum_{i=1}^{\varphi} \sum_{j=1}^{M} (\eta_{\text{wire},ij} E_{\text{wire}} + \eta_{\text{wireless},ij} E_{\text{wireless}} + \eta_{\text{switch},ij} E_{\text{switch}})}{M} \tag{6.2}$$

In (6.2), $\eta_{\text{wire},ij}$, $\eta_{\text{wireless},ij}$, and $\eta_{\text{switch},ij}$ are the numbers of hops the ith flit of the jth message makes on wireline links, wireless links, and the switch stages, respectively. E_{wire}, E_{wireless}, and E_{switch} are the energy dissipated by a flit traversing a single hop on the wired link, wireless link including the WP and a switch, respectively. Finally, M is total number of messages generated.

OPTIMAL CONFIGURATION OF THE SWNoC

The first goal is to determine the suitable maximum number of ports, k_{max}, for the switches of SWNoC. We perform system-level simulations to obtain the optimal values of the parameter k_{max}. The value of $<k>$, the average number of links per switch, is fixed to be 4, which is the same as that of a conventional mesh so that the total number of

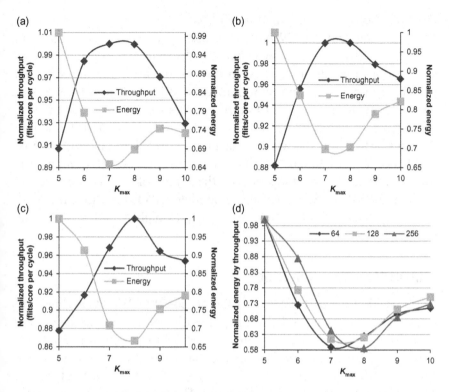

Figure 6.2 (a–c) Normalized throughput and energy and (d) normalized energy by throughput of 64, 128, and 256 system sizes with variation of k_{max} for the SWNoC.

links in the SWNoC is the same as that of a mesh. Fig. 6.2 shows the variation of the throughput, energy, and energy by throughput, with respect to k_{max}, for the different system sizes considered in this chapter, namely, 64, 128, and 256. For each system size, we choose the value of k_{max} which optimizes the energy per throughput as it represents the energy–delay product for each case. From Fig. 6.2, it can be concluded that a k_{max} of 7 optimizes the energy–delay product for 64 and 128 system sizes. For the 256-core system, the suitable value for k_{max} was found to be 8.

It is already shown that in a small-world network, the average hop count decreases with increases in the power law exponent α for a fixed wiring cost (Petermann and De Los Rios, 2005). With $\alpha = 1.8$ used in (3.1), the average hop count is minimum with a fixed wiring cost (Petermann and De Los Rios, 2005). Hence for the results considered in the book, this value for α is selected.

Optimal Configuration of the mSWNoC

We then augment the SWNoC network by adding WIs. Also from Deb et al. (2013), it is shown that the WI placement is most energy efficient when the distance between them is at least 7 mm in the 65-nm technology node. The optimum number of WIs is 12 for a 64-core system size (Wettin et al., 2013a,b). Increasing the number of WIs improves the connectivity of the network as they establish one-hop shortcuts. However, the wireless medium is shared among all the WIs, and hence, as the number of WIs increases beyond a certain limit, performance starts to degrade due to the large token returning period (Deb et al., 2013). Moreover, as the number of WIs increases, the overall energy dissipation from the WIs becomes higher, and it causes the packet energy to increase as well.

THROUGHPUT OF CSWNoC

In this section the performance of the proposed CSWNoC architecture is evaluated in terms of throughput with special emphasis on the behavior in the presence of high rates of failure of the wireless links. First, a uniform random spatial distribution of traffic is considered. Fig. 6.3 shows the variation in throughput with injection load for the CSWNoC for a system size of 64 cores. For comparison, the throughput of a conventional wireline mesh and a SWNoC architecture with all wireline links are also presented. In the SWNoC architecture, all the wired links are pipelined such that between each consecutive stage flits can be transferred in one clock cycle, that is, these links are multi-hop in nature.

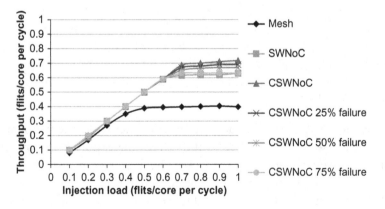

Figure 6.3 Throughput of a 64-core system with variation of injection load.

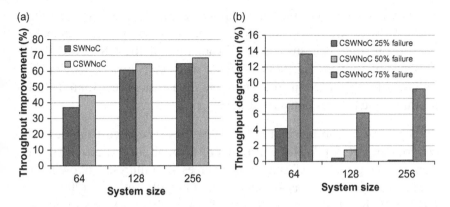

Figure 6.4 (a) Performance improvement of throughput with respect to conventional mesh and (b) performance degradation of throughput with respect to CSWNoC with no failures of same system size.

From Fig. 6.3, we find that the throughput of the CSWNoC is much higher, compared to that of a conventional wireline mesh of the same size. This is because of two reasons: the CSWNoC, being connected following the principles of a small-world network, has a much lower average hop count, and the wireless links connecting the cores separated by long physical distances are through single-hop, low-latency links. The more interesting observation is that, although we inject a high number of wireless link failures by randomly disabling a certain percentage of the wireless links, the throughput does not degrade considerably. This is because the network connectivity is established following a small-world topology.

Fig. 6.4a shows the percentage gain in throughput compared to that of a conventional mesh for a CSWNoC as well as the SWNoC. It can be observed that due to the low average distance between nodes in the small-world topology the performance of the wireline SWNoC is significantly higher compared to that of a mesh. Due to the high-bandwidth and single-hop wireless links, the throughput of the CSWNoC is even higher compared to the wireline SWNoC.

Throughput and Energy Dissipation for CSWNoC With Wireless Link Failure

The throughput is demonstrated for four situations, namely, with no wireless link failure and with 25%, 50%, and 75% of the wireless links failing. The link failure is considered among all wireless links randomly, that is, the probability of failure of any wireless link is same.

For comparison again, the throughput of a conventional wireline mesh and SWNoC are also presented. Fig. 6.4b shows the percentage decrease in the peak sustainable throughput of the CSWNoC in the presence of wireless link failures. Even with high rates of wireless link failures, the degradation in sustainable data rate is less than 15% for all three system sizes considered here.

Next, the performance of the CSWNoC is compared to a hierarchical counterpart, CHWNoC, in terms of throughput at network saturation in the presence of the same degrees of failures. Following the guidelines for best performance in Ganguly et al. (2009), the CHWNoC is considered to have 8 subnets each with 8 cores for a system size of 64, 16 subnets each with 8 cores for a system size of 128, and 16 subnets each with 16 cores for the system size of 256. All the subnets were considered to have mesh-based connectivity among the cores within the subnets.

Fig. 6.5 shows the throughput degradation of the CSWNoC and the CHWNoC along with that of a mesh at network saturation. It is interesting to note that the performance of the CHWNoC degrades comparatively more rapidly than that of the CSWNoC with an increasing degree of failure for the bigger system sizes. For the 64-core system the throughput degradation is almost the same for CSWNoC and CHWNoC. However, for 128- and 256-core systems, while the CSWNoC throughputs degrade by 6.13% and 9.21%, respectively, the corresponding reductions are 35% and 34% for the CHWNoC. The CHWNoC has higher throughput than the wireless CSWNoC in the failure-free case due to the hierarchical structure; however, it has poorer resilience to failure of the wireless links. This correlates to a very insignificant rise in the average hop count in the CSWNoC as shown in Fig. 6.6. The average distance between cores in the CHWNoC, however, increases more with failure of the wireless links. This is because the CHWNoC does not have a perfect small-world topology. The upper level of the hierarchy of the CHWNoC basically has a ring topology with overlaid wireless links. The degradation in the performance for the CHWNoC becomes more apparent for larger system size as failures of wireless links make the upper level dominated by the multihop wired ring architecture. The relative increase in average distance between cores is less with failures for larger system size of the CSWNoC, and hence, the percentage degradation in performance is even less for larger system sizes.

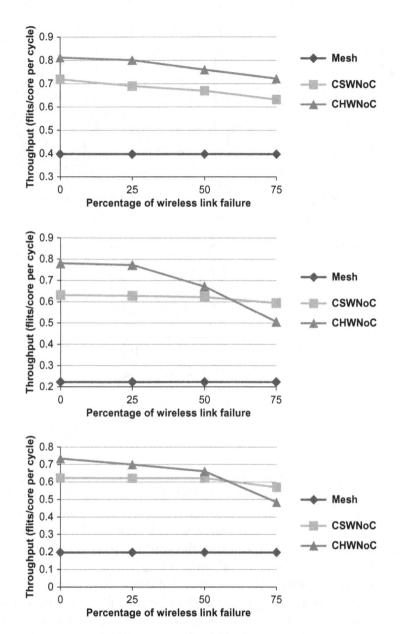

Figure 6.5 Throughput of mesh, CSWNoC, and CHWNoC of system sizes 64, 128, and 256, respectively.

Performance of CSWNoC in the Presence of Nonuniform Traffic

So far only uniform random spatial distribution of traffic has been considered to characterize the performance of the CSWNoC. In reality, however, there could be various different types of traffic

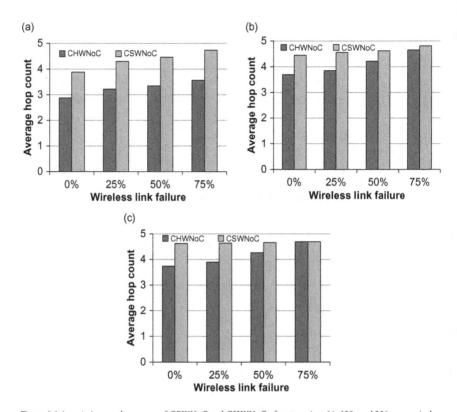

Figure 6.6 (a–c) Average hop count of CSWNoC and CHWNoC of system sizes 64, 128, and 256, respectively.

distributions on the chip depending on the applications considered. In this section the performance of the CSWNoC is presented in the presence of several nonuniform traffic patterns. We consider both synthetic as well as application-specific traffic scenarios on a CSWNoC with 64 cores in this part. Two types of synthetic traffic have been considered to evaluate the performance of the proposed CSWNoC architecture. First, a transpose traffic pattern was considered where each core communicated solely with the core located diametrically opposite to itself on the chip. The other synthetic traffic pattern considered was hotspot, where all the cores in the CSWNoC communicate with a particular core more frequently than with the others. For hotspot, it is assumed that all cores send 10% of the traffic originating in them to a particular core. To model application based traffic, a 256-point fast Fourier transform (FFT) application was considered, wherein each core performs a 4-point radix-2 FFT computation.

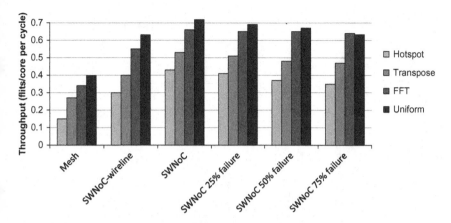

Figure 6.7 Throughput of different traffic types at network saturation.

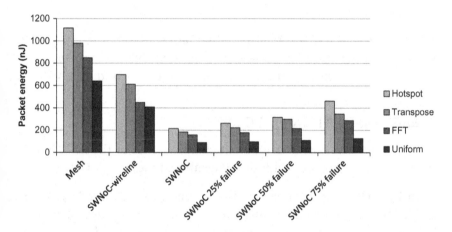

Figure 6.8 Packet energy dissipation of different traffic types at network saturation.

Figs. 6.7 and 6.8 show the maximum throughput and packet energy dissipation, at network saturation of the CSWNoC, in the presence of the same rates of wireless link failures with various types of traffics, respectively. For nonuniform traffic patterns the same trend is maintained following the uniform traffic case. The throughput degrades with increasing amount of wireless links failures, but still, it maintains better performance compared to a flat mesh and the SWNoC. The performance degradations for hotspot and transpose traffic patterns are more than that for FFT. Hotspot and Transpose give rise to more skewed communication patterns; certain links on the path are overloaded and become bottlenecks affecting the overall performance.

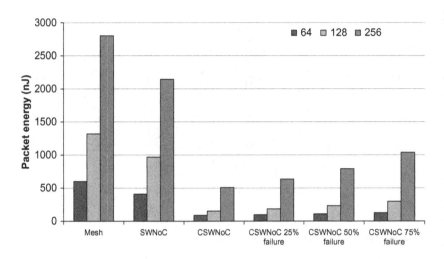

Figure 6.9 Packet energy dissipation of CSWNoC with system size of 64 with mesh for comparison.

The same characteristics hold true for the energy dissipation profile. With increasing number of link failures CSWNoC dissipates more energy, but it still remains below that of the flat mesh and the SWNoC.

ENERGY DISSIPATION FOR CSWNoC

In this section the energy dissipation characteristics of the CSWNoC is evaluated and compared with the conventional mesh architecture.

In Fig. 6.9, the packet energy dissipation of the proposed CSWNoC architecture is compared in the presence of various rates of wireless link failure for the three different system sizes considered in this chapter. For the sake of comparison, the packet energy dissipation of the flat wireline mesh, a SWNoC (small-world NoC where all the links are wireline) are presented, as well as the CSWNoC with wireless links in the presence of various rates of failures. It can be seen that the CSWNoC has significantly lower energy dissipation per packet compared to that of the mesh. To explain the source of savings, we show the various components that contribute to the energy dissipation specifically for the 64-core system in Fig. 6.10.

The two principal contributors of the energy dissipation are the switches and interconnects. In the CSWNoC, the switch power decreases significantly compared to a mesh as a result of the better connectivity of the small world–based architecture. In CSWNoC, the

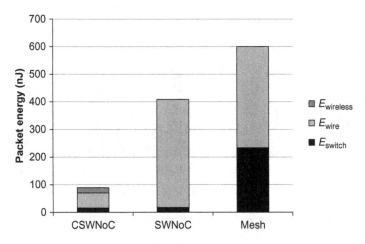

Figure 6.10 Packet energy dissipation components of CSWNoC, SWNoC, and mesh for a system size of 64.

hop count decreases significantly, and hence, the packet has to traverse through less number of switches. In addition, the low−power, long-range wireless links also contribute to a huge savings in energy dissipation, signified by the difference in packet energy between the completely wireline SWNoC and the CSWNoC with the wireless links. As a significant amount of traffic traverses through the wireless channels, the energy dissipated by the wireline part of the interconnects decreases in the CSWNoC. This trend is maintained for the other two system sizes.

In CSWNoC the energy dissipation increases in the presence of large number of wireless link failures as packets need to follow alternative paths. However, the energy dissipation of a CSWNoC with even 75% of wireless link failures is significantly less than that of a mesh and the SWNoC. This demonstrates the resilience of the CSWNoC toward random failures of the wireless interconnections without dissipating significant additional energy.

PACKET LATENCY AND ENERGY DISSIPATION OF mSWNoC

Fig. 6.11 shows the average network latency for the various architectures using the two different routing strategies and considering the abovementioned benchmarks. It can be observed from Fig. 6.11 that for all the benchmarks considered here, the latency of mSWNoC is lower than that of the mesh and SWNoC architectures. This is due to

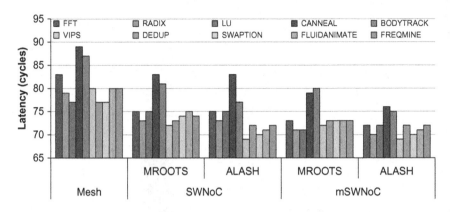

Figure 6.11 Average network latency with various traffic patterns for the Mesh, SWNoC, and mSWNoC architectures.

the small-world, network-based interconnect infrastructure of the mSWNoC with direct long-range wireless links that enables a smaller average hop count than that of mesh and SWNoC (Ganguly et al., 2011; Wettin et al., 2013a,b).

Both the MROOTS and ALASH routing strategies are implemented on the same mSWNoC architecture. The difference in latency arises due to the routing-dependent traffic distribution of the benchmarks. However, it should be noted that the difference in latency among the routing algorithms on the same architecture is small due to the fact that the traffic injection load for all these benchmarks is low and the network operates much below saturation (Gratz and Keckler, 2010). However, the saturation characteristics of mSWNoC in the presence of these routings will be further discussed in the following section.

It can be seen in Fig. 6.11 that MROOTS has a lower latency compared to ALASH for the computation-intensive benchmarks like RADIX, LU, VIPS, DEDUP, SWAPTION, FLUIDANIMATE, and FREQMINE, on both SWNoC and mSWNoC. These benchmarks have traffic injection rates so low, that the root nodes in MROOTS do not encounter enough traffic to become bottlenecks in the routing. As such, MROOTS is able to perform at its best. Without loss of generality, as an example, we show the distribution of flits per switch for one of the computation intensive benchmarks, RADIX, in Fig. 6.12. It can be seen from Fig. 6.12 that ALASH has a larger spread of flit

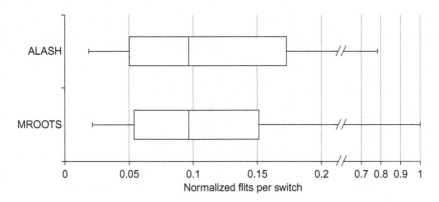

Figure 6.12 Normalized flits per switch distribution for MROOTS and ALASH for the RADIX benchmark.

distribution on the switches (larger difference between the first and third quartiles). This is due to switches that have many links attracting more traffic in ALASH, on average, as they enable a larger number of shortest paths through the network. For MROOTS, only the roots attract high levels of traffic which can be seen in Fig. 6.12 as it has a higher maximum value. It can also be seen in Fig. 6.11 that the latency characteristics for FFT, CANNEAL, and BODYTRACK are reversed and ALASH has a lower latency over MROOTS. For these three benchmarks, the traffic injection rates are high enough that the root switches in MROOTS start to become bottlenecks and performance degradation becomes apparent. The weakness of MROOTS is that there is a strong tendency to generate traffic hotspots near the roots of the spanning trees. The more traffic in the hotspot, the longer messages are delayed in the network due to the root congestion. ALASH does not have a root congestion problem and hence outperforms MROOTS because of the adaptiveness in ALASH for the higher injection load benchmarks.

Fig. 6.13 shows the normalized total network energy dissipation for the mSWNoC, SWNoC, and mesh architectures. We consider the total network energy dissipation to compare the characteristics of the NoC architectures and their associated routing strategies under consideration here. It can be observed from Fig. 6.13 that for each benchmark the network energy is lower for the SWNoC and mSWNoC compared to the mesh architecture. Though the gain in latency for SWNoC/ mSWNoC compared to the mesh is low due to the relatively lower injection loads, the improvement in energy dissipation brings forward

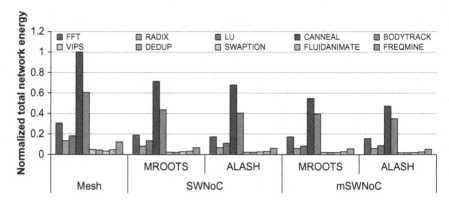

Figure 6.13 Total network energy with various traffic patterns for the Mesh, SWNoC, and mSWNoC architectures.

the benefit of small-world architectures more clearly. The two main contributors of the energy dissipation are from the switches and the interconnect infrastructure. In the SWNoC/mSWNoC, the overall switch energy decreases significantly compared to a mesh as a result of the better connectivity of the architecture. In this case, the hop count decreases significantly, and hence, on the average, packets have to traverse through less number of switches and links. In addition, a significant amount of traffic traverses through energy efficient wireless channels in mSWNoC; consequently allowing the interconnect energy dissipation to be further decreased compared to the SWNoC architecture. It can also be observed from Fig. 6.13 that the energy dissipation for the two different routing strategies follows the same trend as that of the latency. When messages are in the network longer (higher latency) they dissipate more energy. The difference in energy dissipation arising out of the logic circuits of each individual routing is very small and the overall energy dissipation is principally governed by the network characteristics.

Network Saturation Performance of mSWNoC

As mentioned earlier, the benchmarks considered in this work operate below network saturation. To have a detailed comparative performance evaluation of MROOTS and ALASH we also need to see the effects of these routing strategies when the network is in saturation. For this evaluation we artificially inflated the switch interaction rates for the BODYTRACK, CANNEAL, and RADIX benchmarks (a-BODYTRACK, a-CANNEAL, and a-RADIX respectively). Fig. 6.14

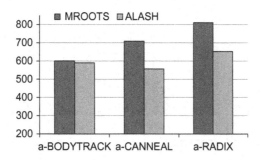

Figure 6.14 Latency in network saturation of the mSWNoC for MROOTS and ALASH running a-BODYTRACK, a-CANNEAL, and a-RADIX.

shows the saturation latency of the MROOTS and ALASH routing strategies using these artificially inflated traffic patterns for mSWNoC. It can be seen from Fig. 6.14 that ALASH performs better than MROOTS. This is due to the inherent problem of any tree-based routing, where the roots of the spanning trees become traffic bottlenecks. As mentioned earlier, when the traffic injection rates are high enough, the root switches start to become traffic hotspots. Hence, the messages get delayed in the network due to root congestion. ALASH does not have a root congestion problem and hence outperforms MROOTS because of the adaptiveness in ALASH. It should be noted that after artificially inflating the computation-intensive benchmark loads, like RADIX, they become more communication intensive. Hence, ALASH outperforms MROOTS in case of a-RADIX.

Thermal Characteristics of mSWNoC

In this section the thermal profile of the mSWNoC, SWNoC, and mesh architectures are evaluated. To quantify the thermal profile of the SWNoC/mSWNoC in the presence of the two routing strategies, the temperatures of the network switches and links are considered. A large focus of this work is to analyze the network characteristics. However, we consider the effects of the processing cores in the HotSpot simulation to accurately portray the temperature-coupling effects that the processors have on their nearby network elements.

We consider the maximum and average switch and link temperature changes between a mesh and SWNoC/mSWNoC, $\Delta T_{\text{hotspot}}$ and ΔT_{avg}, respectively, as the two relevant parameters. As discussed earlier, the benchmarks can be put into two different categories, viz., communication and computation intensive. We consider BODYTRACK

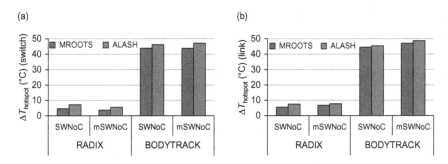

Figure 6.15 Decrease in hotspot (a) switch and (b) link temperatures compared to a mesh for the RADIX and BODYTRACK benchmarks.

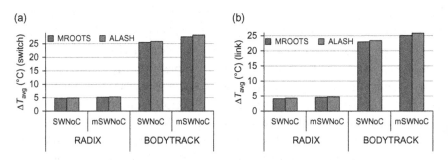

Figure 6.16 Decrease in average (a) switch and (b) link temperatures compared to a mesh for the RADIX and BODYTRACK benchmarks.

and RADIX as two representative examples for the communication- and computation-intensive benchmarks, respectively. However, for the other benchmarks we have observed the same trend. Figs. 6.15 and 6.16 show $\Delta T_{\text{hotspot}}$ and ΔT_{avg} for the links and switches of the two routing strategies, respectively. It can be seen that the SWNoC/ mSWNoC network architectures are inherently much cooler than the mesh counterpart. From Fig. 6.13, we can see that the difference in energy dissipation between the small-world architectures and mesh is significant, and hence, it is natural that SWNoC/mSWNoC switches and links are cooler. Fig. 6.13 helps depict how well each routing strategy performs in distributing the power density, and hence heat, among the network switches and links. This is due to the fact that variations in $\Delta T_{\text{hotspot}}$ correspond to how well the routing mechanism balances the traffic within the network. The more interesting observation while analyzing the temperature profile lies in characterizing the differences among the routing strategies for the small-world architectures. ALASH performs well in distributing the traffic among the network elements. Because of this, ALASH has the lowest maximum network temperature, which can be seen in Fig. 6.15, where ALASH has the largest $\Delta T_{\text{hotspot}}$.

By observing Fig. 6.16, it can also be seen that the average temperature reduction in switches and links among the routing strategies is relatively unaffected. We can conclude that, reduction of the maximum temperature using ALASH has not come at the cost of increasing the average network temperature due to the inherent rerouting efforts of this strategy. Overall, it can be seen that for the routing strategies implemented, we can obtain very similar latency and network energy profiles while reducing the temperature of the hotspot switches and links.

Fig. 6.17 displays the temperature distribution of the switches in the routing schemes of the RADIX and BODYTRACK benchmarks. Here, it can be seen that the MROOTS routing strategy has a larger temperature spread compared to ALASH for both the small-world architectures (the difference between the first and third quartiles is larger). The MROOTS routing strategy will form bottlenecks in the upper levels of its trees, even with a computation-intensive benchmark, such as RADIX, which is demonstrated in Fig. 6.12. In this case, the heat distribution will be spread further as the leaves among the trees see lighter traffic, while the near-root nodes see heavier traffic. ALASH attempts to avoid creating hotspots by having multiple shortest paths. By choosing a path that avoids local network hotspots, we can reduce the maximum network temperature quite well using the ALASH routing strategy. For RADIX and BODYTRACK, ALASH reduces the hotspot switch temperature further compared to MROOTS by 1.86°C and 3.32°C on mSWNoC, respectively.

Between the SWNoC and mSWNoC architectures, the SWNoC achieves a higher switch hotspot temperature reduction for the computation-intensive benchmarks, as their traffic density is small. This can be seen in Fig. 6.17 as SWNoC has a lower maximum temperature over mSWNoC for both routing strategies for the RADIX benchmark. For these benchmarks, the benefits of the wireless shortcuts are outweighed by the amount of traffic that the WIs attract. However, for the communication-intensive benchmarks with higher traffic density, the use of high-bandwidth wireless shortcuts, in the mSWNoC, quickly relieves the higher amount of traffic that the WIs

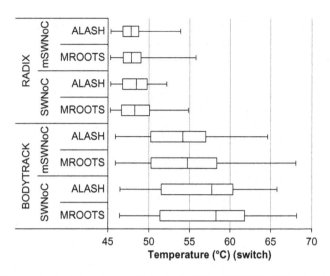

Figure 6.17 Temperature distribution of the switches for the RADIX and BODYTRACK benchmarks.

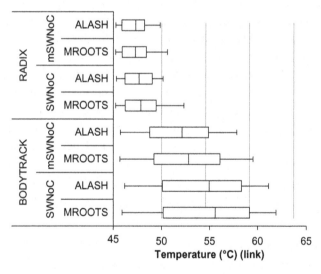

Figure 6.18 Temperature distribution of the links for the RADIX and BODYTRACK benchmarks.

attract. In case of SWNoC, as the shortcuts are implemented through multihop wireline links, moving traffic through these wireline links takes more time and energy which correlates with less temperature reduction. This can be seen in Fig. 6.17 as SWNoC has a higher maximum temperature over mSWNoC for both routing strategies for the BODYTRACK benchmark. Conversely, between SWNoC and mSWNoC, the mSWNoC achieves a higher link hotspot temperature reduction. This is due to the wireless links detouring significant amounts of traffic away from the wireline links.

Fig. 6.18 displays the temperature distribution of the links in the routing schemes of the RADIX and BODYTRACK benchmarks. The links follow the same temperature trend as the switches where the MROOTS routing strategy has a larger temperature spread when compared to ALASH for both the small-world architectures (the difference between first and third quartiles is larger). For RADIX and BODYTRACK, ALASH reduces the hotspot link temperature further compared to MROOTS by 0.92°C and 1.69°C on mSWNoC, respectively.

REFERENCES

Bienia, C., 2011. Benchmarking modern multiprocessors (Ph.D. dissertation). Department of Computer Science, Princeton University, Princeton NJ.

Binkert, N., Beckmann, B., Black, G., Reinhardt, S.K., Saidi, A., Basu, A., et al., 2011. The GEM5 simulator. ACM SIGARCH Comp. Archit. News 39 (2), 1−7.

Chang, K., Deb, S., Ganguly, A., Yu, X., Sah, S.P., Pande, P.P., et al., 2012. Performance evaluation and design trade-offs for wireless network-on-chip architectures. ACM J. Emerg. Technol. Comput. Syst. 8 (3).

Dally, W.J., Towles, B., 2001. Route packets, not wires: on-chip interconnection networks. In: Proceedings of Design Automation Conference, pp. 683−689.

Deb, S., Chang, K., Yu, X., Sah, S., Cosic, M., Ganguly, A., et al., 2013. Design of an energy efficient CMOS compatible NoC architecture with millimeter-wave wireless interconnects. IEEE Trans. Comput. 62 (12), 2382−2396.

Ganguly, A., Chang, K., Pande, P.P., Belzer, B., Nojeh, A., 2009. Performance evaluation of wireless networks on chip architectures. In: Proceedings of ISQED, pp. 350−355.

Ganguly, A., Chang, K., Deb, S., Pande, P.P., Belzer, B., Teuscher, C., 2011. Scalable hybrid wireless network-on-chip architectures for multi-core systems. IEEE Trans. Comput. 60 (10), 1485−1502.

Gratz, P., Keckler, S. Realistic workload characterization and analysis for networks-on-chip design. In: Presented at the 4th Workshop on CMP-MSI, Bangalore, India, January 9, 2010.

Li, S., Ahn, J.H., Strong, R.D., Brockman, J.B., Tullsen, D.M., Jouppi, N.P., 2009. McPAT: an integrated power, area, and timing modeling framework for multicore and manycore architectures. In: Proceedings of MICRO, pp. 469−480.

Petermann, T., De Los Rios, P., 2005. Spatial small-world networks: a wiring cost perspective. arXiv:cond-mat/0501420v2.

Skadron, K., Stan, M.R., Huang, W., Velusamy, S., Sankaranarayanan, K., Tarjan, D., 2003. Temperature-aware microarchitecture. In: Proceedings of ISCA, pp. 2−13.

Wettin, P., Murray, J., Pande, P.P., Shirazi, B., Ganguly, A., 2013a. Energy-efficient multicore chip design through cross-layer approach. In: Proceedings of DATE, pp. 725−730.

Wettin, P., Vidapalapati, A., Ganguly, A., Pande, P.P., 2013b. Complex network enabled robust wireless network-on-chip architectures. ACM J. Emerg. Technol. Comput. Syst. 9 (3), article 24.

Woo, S.C., Ohara, M., Torrie, E., Singh, J.P., Gupta, A., 1995. The SPLASH-2 programs: characterization and methodological considerations. In: Proceedings of ISCA, pp. 24–36.

CHAPTER 7

Dynamic Voltage and Frequency Scaling

The execution flow of a program running on a multicore Network-on-Chip (NoC) generally contains periods of heavy computation followed by periods of intercore data exchange. During periods of high computation, network usage may be at a minimum, allowing the voltage and frequency of links and switches to be tuned down in order to save energy and hence improve the thermal profile while not incurring a significant penalty to network latency. As mentioned previously, presence of memory-bound intervals gives rise to idle cycles in the processing cores that can be exploited to reduce voltage and frequency of the processors as well. By creating a dual-level dynamic voltage and frequency scaling (DVFS) scheme, significant energy savings and subsequent thermal improvements can be achieved to enhance the sustainability of the NoC. The interactions between the processor- and network-level DVFS mechanisms are captured through the simulation process as explained later in this chapter. The following sections describe the processor-level and network-level DVFS implementations adopted in this work.

PROCESSOR-LEVEL DVFS

In this section, the processor-level DVFS technique adopted in this book is described. This technique can be applied individually to each core in a multicore system.

For the processor-level DVFS, compile-time directory flags are inserted into the program before they run on each core. These flags indicate the beginnings of program sections, which could possibly have CPU idle periods. When the program is executed, the DVFS algorithm will not be triggered unless a flag is detected. By combining offline information and runtime behavior, the frequency and voltage can be adjusted precisely.

At the instruction level, the program execution would be suspended mostly on load instructions, pending the completion of the memory-bound operation. Since the goal is to build a fine-grain DVFS scheduling algorithm, focus is on dealing with the load instruction, which can potentially cause CPU idle cycles. This approach is divided into two phases:

- Phase I: Insert directory flags in front of the load instructions that have data references during compilation.

  In phase I, only the load instructions that have data reference dependencies in a pipelined architecture are important. In a pipelined processor architecture, if the required data used for the load instruction is far away from the load, it will not cause any CPU idle time even if the data is not currently stored in the cache. The cache used in the GEM5 (Binkert et al., 2011) setup for these experiments consists of private 64 KB L1 instruction and data caches and shared 64 MB (1 MB distributed per core) L2 cache. An L1 cache hit takes 8 CPU cycles to fetch the data; an L2 cache hit takes at most 32 CPU cycles to fetch the data, and it takes at most 200 cycles to fetch data from main memory. As the data fetched from L1 cache takes 8 cycles, a flag is only inserted in front of such load that the required data will be used within 8 cycles.

- Phase II: The DVFS mechanism is activated only if the processors detect the inserted directory flags during execution of the program.

  In phase II, during program execution, when a flag is detected, the DVFS procedure will keep track of whether the data is fetched. If the data is not fetched within 32 cycles, an L2 cache miss is detected. Similarly, a main memory miss, which could be caused by locks or barriers in the program, will be detected if the data is not back within 200 cycles. Once an L2 or higher order memory miss is detected, frequency and voltage will be decreased by one step. During a voltage transition, additional memory misses are ignored. After a particular transition is complete, additional memory misses allow the voltage/frequency to step down further. On the contrary, once all of the required data has been fetched and no more data misses have been detected until that time, voltage and frequency will be increased by one step until the voltage and frequency are returned to their maximum values; otherwise the CPU state remains the same even if the data has been fetched. This is reasonable because although the previous data has come back, new potential idle time may have been detected. When DVFS is applied, if the execution time of a benchmark is very short, voltage/frequency transition time may take a considerable portion of the total execution time. Therefore, the power and delay overheads arising due to the incorporation of DVFS will be significant for benchmarks with short execution times. In this case, the number of voltage/frequency changes has to be reduced in order to get a reasonable energy–delay trade-off.

Suppose the execution time T of the benchmark is known (T can be obtained from profiling the program using GEM5), the algorithm should be improved to satisfy the following two criterions:

(1) There exists T_0, such that when the program execution time T exceeds T_0, then the above-mentioned DVFS mechanism can be applied as is.
(2) The shorter the execution time T is, the voltage/frequency should be allowed to switch less frequently. When a data miss is detected, the DVFS controller waits for an additional number of cycles equal to ΔT before reducing CPU voltage and frequency. In other words, the total waiting time is $\Delta T + 32$ cycles (L2 cache miss) or $\Delta T + 200$ cycles (main memory miss). If the data is fetched within the waiting time, voltage and frequency will not be reduced. The additional waiting time, ΔT, is inversely proportional to the execution time T.

$$\Delta T = k/T \tag{7.1}$$

According to Criterion (1), ΔT is less than 1 if and only if $T > T_0$. Thus, we obtain:

$$\begin{aligned} k/T_0 &= 1 \\ k &= T_0 \end{aligned} \tag{7.2}$$

By substituting (7.2) in (7.1) we get the final expression of ΔT:

$$\Delta T = T_0/T \tag{7.3}$$

The methodology to determine suitable values of T_0 will be discussed later in this chapter.

NETWORK-LEVEL DVFS

The wireless links in the millimeter-wave SWNoC (mSWNoC) establish one-hop shortcuts between the far apart switches and facilitate energy savings in data exchange. By reducing the hop count between largely separated communicating cores, wireless shortcuts have been shown to attract a significant amount of the overall traffic within the network. The amount of traffic detoured is substantial and the low-power wireless links enable energy savings. However, the overall energy dissipation within the network is still dominated by the data traversing the wireline links (Deb et al., 2012). Hence, we propose to incorporate DVFS on these wireline links to save more energy. In this scheme, every NoC router predicts future traffic patterns based on what was seen in the past. The metric to determine whether DVFS should be performed is link utilization. The short-term link utilization is characterized by (7.4).

$$U_{\text{Short}} = \frac{1}{H} \sum_{i=1}^{H} f_i \qquad (7.4)$$

where H is the history window and f_i is 1 if a flit traversed the link on the ith cycle of the history window and a 0 otherwise. The predicted future link utilization, $U_{\text{Predicted}}$, is an exponential weighted average determined for each link according to (7.5).

$$U_{\text{Predicted}} = \frac{W \cdot U_{\text{Short}} + U_{\text{Predicted}}}{W + 1} \qquad (7.5)$$

where W is the weight given to the short-term utilization over the long-term utilization. After T cycles have elapsed, where $1/T$ is the maximum allowable switching rate, the router determines whether a given link's predicted utilization meets a specific threshold. By allowing thresholds at several different levels of $U_{\text{Predicted}}$, a finer-grain balance between energy savings, due to lowering the voltage and frequency, and latency penalty, due to mispredictions and voltage/frequency transitions, can be obtained.

Lee et al. (2007) elaborates the need for a Power Management Unit to control supply voltage and clock to tune voltage and frequency, respectively. Voltage regulators and frequency converters are required to step-up or step-down voltages and frequencies in order to dynamically adjust each, respectively. A comparative study of various schemes can be seen in Usman et al. (2013). By following Kim et al. (2008), and using on-chip voltage regulators, transition time can be reduced drastically.

Similar to Shang et al. (2002), a DVFS algorithm was developed using (7.4) and (7.5). After T cycles, the algorithm determines if DVFS should be performed on the link based on the predicted bandwidth requirements of future traffic. Depending on which threshold was crossed, if any, the router then determines whether to tune the voltage and frequency of the link. In order to prevent a direct multithreshold jump, which would cause high delay, the voltage and frequency can step up once, step down once, or remain unchanged during one voltage/frequency transition. After each adjustment of the voltage/frequency pair on a given link, energy savings and latency penalty were determined. The energy of the link, E_{link}, was determined by (7.6)

$$E_{link} = \sum_{T} N_{flits} \cdot E_{flit} \cdot V_T^2 \qquad (7.6)$$

where N_{flits} is the number of flits over the period T, E_{flit} is the energy per flit of the link, and V_T is the DVFS-scaled voltage for the given period. The total energy of the link is summed over all switching periods within the entire simulation period.

Latency penalty due to DVFS is composed of the following two main factors:

(1) A misprediction penalty is caused when the adjusted voltage/frequency pair do not meet the bandwidth requirements of the traffic over the given switching interval. The bandwidth requirement of the link is obtained by viewing the current link utilization over a smaller window whose size is determined as the average latency of a flit in the non-DVFS network. An example of the misprediction penalty during a snapshot of the FFT benchmark can be seen in Fig. 7.1, where each bar represents the link utilization over an N-cycle window. If the bar is higher than the threshold line, the bandwidth requirements of the flits traversed in that window are not met. This results in a latency penalty for the flits in that N-cycle window. This penalty can be considered the worst case, as it assumes that every flit is time-critical, and a processor may be able to progress after the flit arrives.

(2) Adjusting the voltage/frequency pair on the link causes a switching penalty. A transition delay of 100 ns was accounted for according to Kim et al. (2008). During this transition, we conservatively do not attempt to send any information on the link.

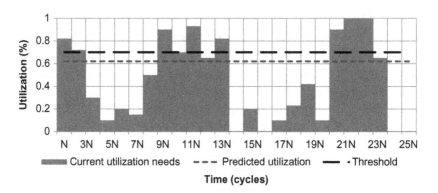

Figure 7.1 DVFS link latency penalty determination.

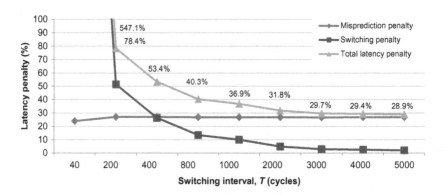

Figure 7.2 Latency penalty versus switching window size of a link (FFT).

To determine the appropriate switching window, the misprediction penalties and switching penalties are found on all wireline links. Fig. 7.2 shows the total latency penalty in the presence of FFT traffic while varying T. The other benchmarks also show the same trend. A small switching window may catch data bursts, which do not represent a long-term trend of the benchmark's traffic. Consequently, widely varying short-term traffic utilizations, which can be seen in Fig. 7.1, will cause the voltage/frequency to change often. As seen in Fig. 7.2, for small switching windows, there is a large penalty due to frequently changing the voltage/frequency pair of the link. As the switching window widens, the switch penalty reduces drastically, while the overhead due to latency penalty increases slowly. A switching window size of $T = 5000$ was selected as the benefits of a larger window size beyond that were minimal.

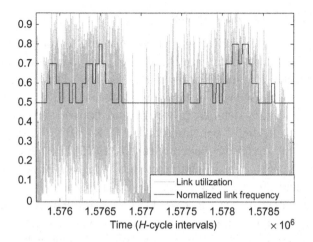

Figure 7.3 Sample FFT frequency tracking.

From Fig. 7.3, it can be seen that the link frequency tracks the utilization over an H-cycle window. We scale our voltage/frequency after T cycles have elapsed in order to prevent large latency penalties due to frequency switching. This method will attempt to predict the next T cycles correctly by tracking the utilization of the link over time.

By using on-chip voltage regulators with fast transitions, latency penalties and energy overheads due to voltage transitions can be kept low. We estimate the energy overhead introduced by the regulators due to voltage transition as:

$$E_{\text{regulator}} = (1 - \eta) \cdot C_{\text{filter}} \cdot \left| V_2^2 - V_1^2 \right| \qquad (7.7)$$

where $E_{\text{regulator}}$ is the energy dissipated by the voltage regulator due to a voltage transition, η is the power efficiency of the regulator, C_{filter} is the regulator filter capacitance, and V_2 and V_1 are the two voltage levels. A multithreshold jump between voltage/frequency pairs will result in a high switching delay. Thus, only single threshold transitions are allowed. The switching penalty is a result of having to tune the voltage. We conservatively allow the voltage to transition between states without performing instructions on the effected CPU or transmitting data over the effected wireline link during that time. Hence, during a switch between states, the processor or wireline link incurs a 100-ns penalty (Kim et al., 2008).

PERFORMANCE EVALUATION

In this section, we evaluate the performance and temperature profile of the mSWNoC and compare those with the conventional wireline mesh-based NoC by incorporating the dual-level DVFS elaborated in this chapter. As discussed in Chapter 6, we use GEM5, a full system simulator, to obtain detailed processor and network-level information A subset of SPLASH-2 benchmarks, FFT, RADIX, LU (Woo et al., 1995), and the PARSEC benchmark CANNEAL (Bienia, 2011) are considered as they vary in characteristics from computation intensive to communication intensive in nature and thus are of particular interest in this work. Processor-level DVFS is implemented within the GEM5 simulator to obtain accurate execution time penalties and performance statistics when different parts of the benchmark are run with various voltage/frequency pairs. The processor-level statistics generated by GEM5 simulations are incorporated into McPAT (Multi-core Power, Area, and Timing) (Li et al., 2009) to determine the processor-level power statistics.

After obtaining processor and network power values, the processors and the network switches and links are arranged on a 20-mm × 20-mm die. These floor plans, along with the power values, are used in HotSpot (Skadron et al., 2003) to obtain steady-state thermal profiles. The architecture-dependent core powers and their corresponding network powers with and without DVFS in the presence of the specific benchmarks are fed to the HotSpot simulator to obtain the temperature profiles of each scenario. The flow of the overall simulation process is shown in Fig. 7.4.

As temperature is closely related to the energy dissipation of the chip, the thermal profile depends on the energy dissipation of the processors and the network infrastructure, which will be quantified shortly. To compare the characteristics of the thermal profiles of a particular region in the chip, the average communication density and computation density are considered. These are defined by (7.8) and (7.9), respectively,

$$\rho_{comm} = \frac{1}{t_c} \left[\sum_i \frac{N_{fs_i}}{N_{switch}} + \sum_j \frac{N_{fl_j}}{N_{link}} \right] \qquad (7.8)$$

$$\rho_{\text{comp}} = \frac{1}{t_c} \sum_k \frac{N_{\text{ic}_k}}{N_{\text{core}}} \tag{7.9}$$

where ρ_{comm} is the average communication density in flits per cycle (FPC) over the region of interest. ρ_{comp} is the average computation density in instructions per cycle (IPC) over the region of interest. N_{switch}, N_{link}, and N_{core} are the number of switches, links, and cores in the region of interest, respectively. N_{fr}, N_{fl}, and N_{ic} are the number of flits traveled on each switch and link in that region, and the number of instructions performed on each core in that region, respectively. The total number of cycles executed is t_c. If the average communication and computation densities of a given area on the chip are high, the temperature in that region will also be correspondingly high.

First, we discuss the features of the mSWNoC architecture and then we present its latency, energy dissipation, and thermal characteristics by incorporating dual-level DVFS.

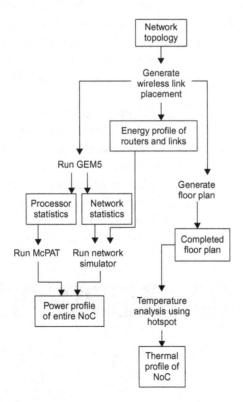

Figure 7.4 Simulation flow.

DVFS Setup

Both the processor- and network-level DVFS algorithms require tuning of the relevant parameters described in the earlier sections of this chapter in order to optimize the benefits of performing DVFS. First, the parameters of the processor-level DVFS algorithm are optimized. To do this, the idle/busy cycles of the processing cores while running various benchmarks need to be analyzed. Table 7.1 shows the percentage of busy/idle cycles for the benchmarks evaluated. This indicates the opportunity to save power while running an application. If there are more idle cycles, then there is more opportunity to save processor-level power because we can reduce the frequency/voltage during those idle cycles while causing minimal effects on the performance. For example, the CANNEAL benchmark provides us with more opportunity to turn down frequency and voltage of the processing cores without effecting performance compared to the SPLASH-2 benchmarks.

Next, the characteristics of the DVFS mechanisms proposed earlier are analyzed for different benchmarks. Table 7.2 shows the energy savings and latency (execution time) penalties for the cores in the presence of the original and delayed DVFS algorithms. In the rows of "Penalty/ Savings," positive numbers represent a penalty while negative numbers represent savings. Obviously the performance of the original DVFS algorithm for the FFT benchmark is much worse than the other benchmarks. We not only pay 26% latency penalty but also dissipate 23% more energy. For all the other benchmarks, although we pay latency penalties, we achieve energy savings. Based on these results, the considered DVFS strategy can be improved as follows. The principal difference between FFT and the other benchmarks is the total execution time. The execution time of the FFT benchmark is significantly less than the others. Hence, the execution time dependence expressed in (7.1)–(7.3) is incorporated into the DVFS mechanism.

Table 7.1 Percentage of Busy and Idle Cycles in a 64-Core System Given Default Problem Sizes			
Benchmark	Busy (%)	Idle (%)	Default Problem Size
FFT	81.99	18.01	65,536 Data Points
RADIX	84.98	15.02	262,144 Integers, 1024 RADIX
LU	87.62	12.38	512 × 512 Matrix, 16 × 16 Blocks
CANNEAL	56.74	43.26	200,000 Elements

Table 7.2 Energy Savings Versus Latency Penalty of Processor-Level DVFS Algorithms

	FFT		RADIX		LU		CANNEAL	
	Exec. Time (s)	Energy (J)	Exec. Time (s)	Energy (J)	Exec. Time (s)	Energy (J)	Exec. Time (s)	Energy (J)
No DVFS	0.003172	0.0881	0.064782	1.72233	0.092254	2.96353	0.143129	3.92351
Original DVFS	0.003987	0.10678	0.073981	1.55597	0.103724	2.83343	0.150872	3.19681
Penalty/savings	25.69%	23.20%	14.20%	−9.75%	12.43%	−4.39%	5.41%	−18.52%
Delayed DVFS	0.003421	0.08398	0.068432	1.53252	0.103168	2.58755	0.150872	3.19681
Penalty/savings	7.85%	−4.68%	5.63%	−11.02%	11.83%	−12.69%	5.41%	−18.52%

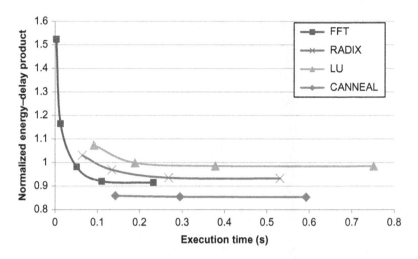

Figure 7.5 Normalized energy–delay product of benchmarks with various problem sizes with original processor-level DVFS algorithm.

The influence of execution time needs to be quantified so as to set the threshold T_0. Fig. 7.5 shows the normalized energy–delay product for the four benchmarks as a function of the execution time with different problem sizes after applying the original DVFS algorithm. The problem size is increased by a factor of 2 from the default scenario shown in Table 7.1 until the variation in the energy–delay product becomes steady. It can be seen that if the program execution time is roughly more than 0.2 s, then the energy–delay product becomes almost steady with respect to the execution time. Therefore, the suitable value of T_0 used in (7.3) is 0.2 s. It should also be noted for the default problem size, the execution times for the LU and RADIX benchmarks are also significantly less than 0.2 s and hence the delayed DVFS algorithm performs better for them also. For the standard problem size CANNEAL, the execution time is an order of magnitude higher than that of the others (very close to 0.2 s). Therefore, for CANNEAL, both DVFS mechanisms offer the same performance benefits.

In our experiments, the energy–delay trade-offs are evaluated by varying the waiting time between reducing voltage/frequency and flag detection. The waiting time, T_{wait}, is determined by (7.10),

$$T_{\text{wait}} = \gamma \cdot T_{\text{original}} \qquad (7.10)$$

where γ is the control factor, and T_{original} is the total waiting time discussed in the Processor-Level DVFS section above. To be specific,

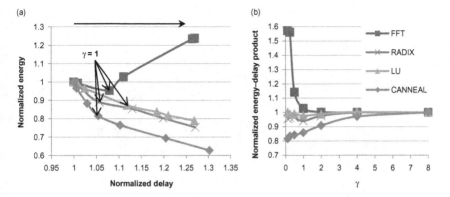

Figure 7.6 (a) Energy–delay trade-off and (b) energy–delay product with varying γ for processor-level DVFS.

$T_{\text{original}} = 32 + \Delta T$ in case of an L2 cache miss, and $T_{\text{original}} = 168 + \Delta T$ for a main memory miss after an L2 cache miss has been detected. Generally, a lower value for γ will result in more energy savings with a larger latency penalty. Fig. 7.6a and b show the energy versus delay and the energy–delay products of processor-level DVFS with different values of γ for the four benchmarks considered in this chapter. From Fig. 7.6a, it is evident that as γ is decreased, energy savings increases at the expense of execution time, with the exception of the FFT benchmark. The FFT benchmark, as discussed above, does not allow much opportunity to control the energy–delay trade-off. Due to its short execution time, if we apply a small γ, voltage and frequency transitions are scheduled too frequently, and hence, the switching penalty becomes a dominating factor. This causes both energy dissipation and execution time to increase. On the other hand, as ΔT is high for FFT, γ greater than 1 will have little opportunity to perform DVFS due to the long waiting time. Thus, for FFT, the highest energy savings is obtained at $\gamma = 1$. For RADIX and LU, it can be seen in Fig. 7.6b that the energy–delay product is minimized when $\gamma = 1$. The CANNEAL benchmark represents a program with a long execution time, and a significant opportunity to save energy. From Fig. 7.6b, it can be seen that minimizing γ also minimizes the energy–delay product. However, this comes at a significantly higher execution time penalty. Tuning these parameters allows users the opportunity to choose their system requirements, whether it is high-energy savings, low execution time penalty, or a minimized energy–delay product. Therefore, in our experiments, $\gamma = 1$ is utilized, as it provides energy savings for a reasonable time penalty for all of the benchmarks considered.

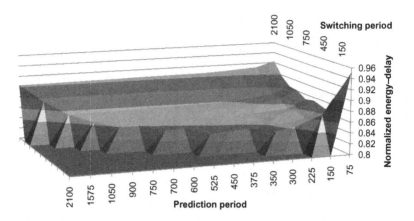

Figure 7.7 Energy–delay product versus switching and prediction periods of a link.

Next, the parameters of the network-level DVFS algorithm are optimized. First, to determine the appropriate prediction and switching windows of the network-level DVFS, we consider the network-level energy–delay product by varying these two parameters. The optimum point is found for all the benchmarks considered in this work, and as an example the LU benchmark is plotted in Fig. 7.7. A small switching window may catch data bursts, which do not represent a long-term trend of the benchmark's traffic. Consequently, widely varying short-term traffic utilizations will cause the voltage/frequency to change often. In this case, the regulator energy overhead may outweigh the benefits of a lower misprediction penalty. As the switching window widens, the regulator energy overhead impact is decreased, while the latency penalty increases. A switching window of $T = 450$ cycles, and a history window of $H = 450$ cycles were selected for all the SPLASH-2 benchmarks, as this optimizes the energy–delay trade-off for them. For CANNEAL, however, $T = H = 900$ cycles. Similarly, the weight parameter, W, defined in (7.5) was chosen to be 2 for all benchmarks as it optimized the energy–delay product.

From Fig. 7.8, it can be seen that the link frequency tracks the utilization over an H-cycle window. The voltage/frequency is scaled after T cycles have elapsed in order to prevent large latency penalties due to frequency switching. This method will attempt to predict the next T cycles correctly by tracking the utilization of the link over time. The selected voltage/frequency pairs corresponding to each level of DVFS are shown in Table 7.3. Based on the required busy percentages of the

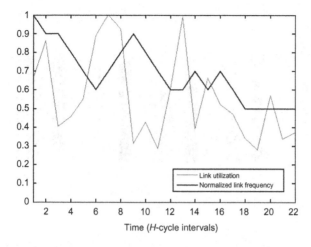

Figure 7.8 Sample LU frequency tracking.

Table 7.3 Voltage/Frequency/Threshold Combinations		
Voltage (V)	**Frequency (GHz)**	**Threshold**
1	2.5	≥ 0.9
0.9	2.25	≥ 0.8
0.8	2.0	≥ 0.7
0.7	1.75	≥ 0.6
0.6	1.5	≥ 0.5
0.5	1.25	< 0.5

cores and bandwidth thresholds of the wireline links as a fraction of the maximum allowable value, these scaled voltage/frequency pairs were determined.

Execution Time Penalty

In this section, how the proposed dual-level DVFS-enabled mSWNoC architecture affects the overall execution time is evaluated. The execution time directly relates to the latency penalty. Fig. 7.9 shows the average packet latency within only the network. We show the latency for mesh, DVFS-enabled mesh, mSWNoC, and DVFS-enabled mSWNoC. It is clear that mSWNoC offers less latency than the original mesh architecture. The latency improvement introduced by the mSWNoC is essentially balanced with the penalty introduced by the network-level DVFS. Consequently, the overall execution time penalty will arise as a

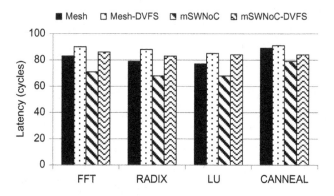

Figure 7.9 Average packet latency of mesh and mSWNOC with and without DVFS.

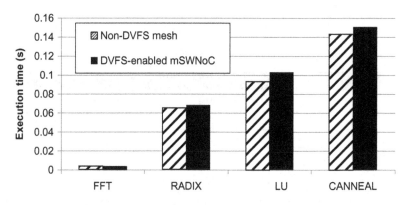

Figure 7.10 Overall execution time.

worst case, by considering the execution time penalty introduced by the processor-level DVFS algorithm. Fig. 7.10 shows the execution time of the dual-level DVFS-enabled mSWNoC compared with the non-DVFS standard mesh architecture. The execution time penalty due to DVFS in the presence of FFT, RADIX, LU, and CANNEAL traffics are 8%, 6%, 12%, and 5%, respectively, over the non-DVFS mesh. As mentioned above, this penalty is due to the DVFS algorithm implemented on the processing cores. The network does not contribute to the overall execution time penalty due to its efficient architecture. The penalties that arise from the tested benchmarks are relatively similar.

Energy Dissipation

In this section, the energy dissipation characteristics of the proposed mSWNoC architecture in the presence of the dual-level DVFS is

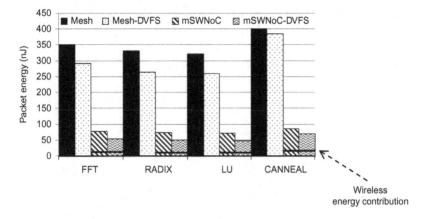

Figure 7.11 Average packet energy of mesh and mSNoC with and without DVFS.

evaluated. Fig. 7.11 shows the packet energy dissipation for both the mSWNoC and mesh architectures. The packet energy dissipation is defined as the average energy dissipated in transmitting one packet between source and destination switches, thereby reflecting the network characteristics. The contribution from wireless energy dissipation of the mSWNoC is the portion of energy below the bolded horizontal lines in Fig. 7.11. While determining the packet energy in the presence of DVFS, the energy overhead due to the voltage regulators are incorporated by considering η to be 0.77 and C_{filter} to be 5 nF according to Kudva and Harjani (2011).

From Fig. 7.11, we can observe that the mSWNoC architecture provides a significant reduction in network energy. The two contributors of the network energy dissipation are from the switches and the interconnect infrastructure. In the mSWNoC, the overall switch energy decreases significantly compared to a mesh as a result of the better connectivity of the architecture. In this case, the hop count decreases significantly and hence the packet has to traverse through less number of switches and links. In addition, a significant amount of traffic traverses through the energy-efficient wireless channels, consequently allowing the interconnect energy dissipation to decrease. By implementing DVFS, for both the architectures, energy savings are obtained. The network-level energy savings between mesh and DVFS-enabled mesh vary between 4% for CANNEAL and 21% for RADIX. Between the mSWNoC and DVFS-enabled mSWNoC the savings are between 18% for CANNEAL and 33% for LU. As the mSWNoC

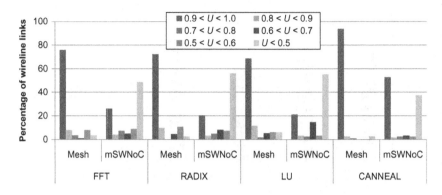

Figure 7.12 Wireline link utilization histogram.

architecture lowers the amount of traffic traversing the wired links, there is more opportunity to perform DVFS on the mSWNoC architecture. A histogram of the wireline link level traffic utilizations is shown in Fig. 7.12. From this, it is clear that in the mesh architecture, a significant amount of links have more than 90% utilization for the considered benchmarks, and hence, the savings in energy are lower. In this case, there is not significant room for improvement with DVFS as the voltage and frequency cannot be tuned often on the links with high utilization. On the other hand, the mSWNoC reduces traffic on wireline links as the wireless channels carry a significant amount of traffic, which can also be seen clearly in Fig. 7.12. As the majority of wireline links fall under 50% utilization in the mSWNoC architecture, there is a significant opportunity for implementing DVFS. Because of this, there is room for more energy savings in mSWNoC in the presence of DVFS compared to the mesh architecture.

Fig. 7.13 shows the total energy savings of the dual-level DVFS mSWNoC architecture over the non-DVFS mesh architecture. As discussed above, the execution time greatly affects the amount of DVFS performed in the delayed DVFS algorithm on the processors. As such, and coupled with the idle cycle availability shown in Table 7.1, the SPLASH-2 benchmarks have less opportunity for energy savings. As mentioned above, the extremely short execution time of the FFT benchmark limits its DVFS performance, and hence processor-level energy savings to 5%. When the execution time increases toward T_0, as seen in the CANNEAL benchmark, the processor-level energy savings nears 20%. From Fig. 7.13, a clear trend can be seen. The contribution from the cores significantly dominates the overall energy dissipation.

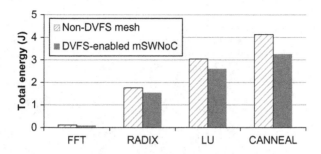

Figure 7.13 Energy savings of dual-level DVFS mSWNoC versus non-DVFS mesh architecture.

By viewing the energy savings of only the network, between non-DVFS mesh and DVFS-enabled mSWNoC, we can see a relatively constant amount of savings across the benchmarks. In the FFT benchmark, while the processor-level DVFS only saves around 5% of the overall processor energy, the network energy makes up 22% of the total energy. As such, the 81% energy savings in the network of the DVFS-enabled mSWNoC over the non-DVFS mesh allows for the total energy savings to be 21%. The total energy savings for the other benchmarks are 12%, 14%, and 21% for RADIX, LU, and CANNEAL, respectively, due to the relatively lower savings in the processor energy dissipation compared to the network. In the CANNEAL scenario, as the core idle percentage is higher, the opportunity for DVFS among the cores is greater. Thus, the total energy savings in CANNEAL is greater as the core savings has increased. Realistically, as there are scenarios of high network energy and low computational energy and vice versa, this demonstrates the need to implement DVFS within both the processors and the network in order to maximize potential energy savings.

Thermal Hotspots

In this section, the thermal hotspot issues for the benchmarks considered are elaborated and relate it to the computation and communication densities. For the purpose of demonstration, we consider one SPLASH-2 benchmark (LU) and one PARSEC benchmark (CANNEAL) as they have the temperature hotspot issues in both the processing cores and the network. Fig. 7.14a and b shows the HotSpot thermal plots for the LU benchmark in the non-DVFS mesh and dual-level DVFS-enabled mSWNoC, respectively. Here, it can be seen that within the LU benchmark, a single core has become the hotspot, with

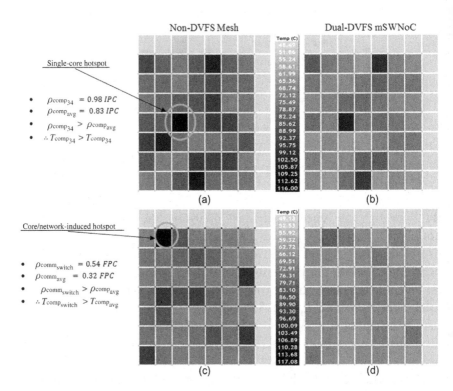

Figure 7.14 HotSpot thermal plots of (a) non-DVFS mesh LU, (b) dual-level DVFS mSWNoC LU, (c) non-DVFS mesh CANNEAL, and (d) dual-level DVFS mSWNoC CANNEAL.

several other cores also near the hotspot temperature. This is a worst-case scenario, as it displays an imbalance in the computation densities of the tasks distributed among the cores. The core in question, core 34, has a computation density of 0.98 IPC, which is higher than the average computation density of 0.83 IPC among the cores in the LU benchmark. As the computational density of core 34 is higher than the average, the core's energy is significantly higher than any other core that is not directly along the chip edge. This results in a hotspot formed at that specific core. By enabling dual-level DVFS on the mSWNoC, the temperature of the hotspot location was reduced by 11.06°C. Fig. 7.14c and d shows the HotSpot thermal plot for the CANNEAL benchmark in the non-DVFS mesh and dual-level DVFS-enable mSWNoC, respectively. In this scenario, the hotspot temperature in the network is as high as the hotspot temperature in the processing cores. This introduces a network-induced hotspot among the chip. In this scenario, the switch in question has a large communication density (0.54 FPC), larger than the average communication density of the switches in the network (0.32 FPC). Performing DVFS and switching to the mSWNoC architecture reduces the average communication density of the network switches to 0.13 FPC. However, the hotspot switch increased in communication density (0.69 FPC) as its wireless shortcut becomes a traffic attractor. However, the temperature of the hotspot location is reduced by 26.30°C. This phenomenon occurs because of the massive reduction in neighboring core temperatures after processor-level DVFS. As the hotspot core temperatures reduce drastically, the heat dissipated to the nearby switches is also reduced, and hence, there is temperature savings in the switches. For the mesh architecture without DVFS, the hotspot switch temperature is 116.1°C, with neighboring core temperatures of 47.38°C, 47.36°C, 117.1°C, and 86.13°C. Because the hotspot core (117.1°C) is neighboring the switch, a lot of heat is dissipated onto the switch. This can be seen by observing the same hotspot switch after enabling dual-level DVFS. In this case, the neighboring core temperatures are 46.92°C, 47.00°C, 83.25°C, and 75.91°C, and the switch temperature is reduced by 25.32−90.78°C. This large change in temperature is largely caused by the heat transfer from the hotspot core to that switch.

Temperature Profile

In this section, we evaluate the thermal profile of the mSWNoC incorporating dual-level DVFS. In Fig. 7.15 we present the number of cores within particular temperature ranges for the different benchmarks. Here, it can be seen that the DVFS-enabled mSWNoC allows the temperature among the cores to decrease. This is evident from Fig. 7.15 and shown by the leftward shift in the histograms of core temperatures among the benchmarks.

As a specific example, in the presence of CANNEAL traffic, it can be seen that cores with temperatures above 90°C in the mesh architecture without DVFS are shifted to the lower temperature ranges after implementing dual-level DVFS on the mSWNoC architecture. The average reduction in core temperature between non-DVFS mesh and dual-level DVFS mSWNoC, ΔT_{avg}, is 5.93°C. This is also shown in Table 7.4. Similarly, for FFT, RADIX, and LU benchmarks, it can be seen that cores are also shifted to the lower temperature ranges after implementing dual-level DVFS. The average reductions in core temperatures between dual-level, DVFS-enabled mSWNoC and the

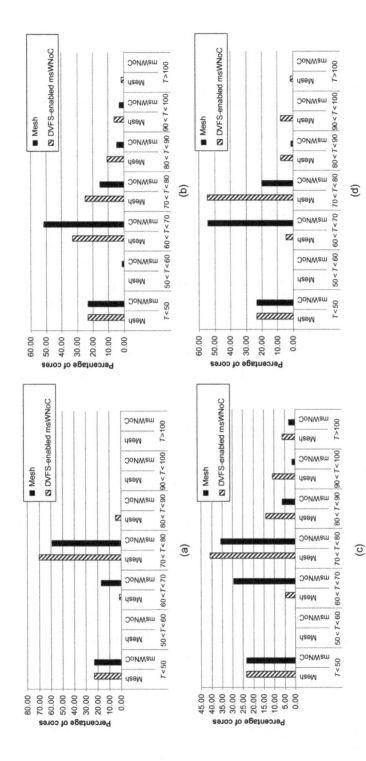

Figure 7.15 Thermal histograms of cores: (a) FFT, (b) RADIX, (c) LU, and (d) CANNEAL.

Table 7.4 Change in Core Temperatures Between Non-DVFS Mesh and Dual-Level DVFS mSWNoC

	FFT (°C)	RADIX (°C)	LU (°C)	CANNEAL (°C)
ΔT_{avg}	2.78	3.80	5.93	5.93
ΔT_{max}	1.47	17.04	11.10	33.85
$\Delta T_{hotspot}$	1.18	17.04	11.10	33.85

non-DVFS mesh for all the benchmarks are shown in Table 7.4. As an example, as shown in Fig. 7.15c, nearly 10% of the 64 cores which were above 90°C were decreased to temperatures between 60°C and 90°C when performing dual-level DVFS on the CANNEAL benchmark. To quantify the improvement in the thermal profile by incorporating dual-level DVFS on the mSWNoC, we consider two parameters. The first parameter is the difference in maximum core temperature between the dual-level DVFS mSWNoC and the non-DVFS mesh and is denoted as $\Delta T_{hotspot}$. The second parameter ΔT_{max} is the reduction in the temperature of the core that initially was hottest. Values of both $\Delta T_{hotspot}$ and ΔT_{max} for all the benchmarks are displayed in Table 7.4. As both these parameters are positive, the temperature of the hottest core with no DVFS is being drastically reduced (removing the original hotspot), and the new maximum core temperature is also being reduced. In the FFT benchmark, the change in hotspot temperature is small because the benchmark offers little opportunity to perform DVFS as described earlier. As mentioned above, while the overall energy savings of FFT is large, this is due to the network owning a larger percentage of overall energy for this benchmark. Thus, if the hotspots reside in the processing cores, and the savings in energy in the processing cores is low, the hotspot will not cool much. RADIX, LU, and CANNEAL have much higher opportunities for hotspot temperature savings as those benchmarks have longer execution times and, hence, more opportunities for DVFS. As an example, in the case of the CANNEAL benchmark the non-DVFS mesh creates core temperatures as high as 117.1°C. This might compromise chip reliability, as it will give rise to a thermal emergency (Sankaranarayanan et al., 2005). The dual-level DVFS implementation produces a hottest core temperature of 83.25°C. Consequently, thermal emergencies are averted.

The thermal characteristics of the network are shown in Fig. 7.16. As mentioned above, the chosen benchmarks vary from highly

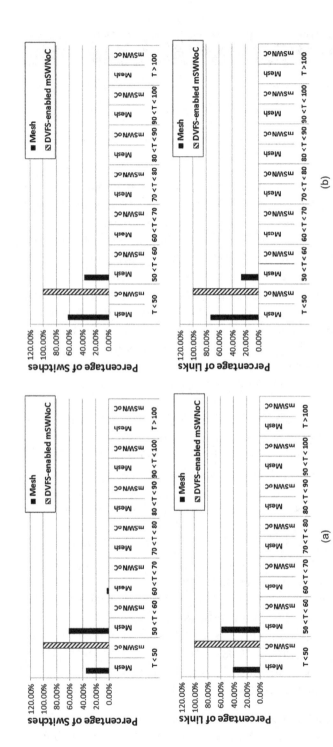

Figure 7.16 Thermal histogram of switches and wireline link segments: (a) FFT, (b) RADIX, (c) LU, and (d) CANNEAL.

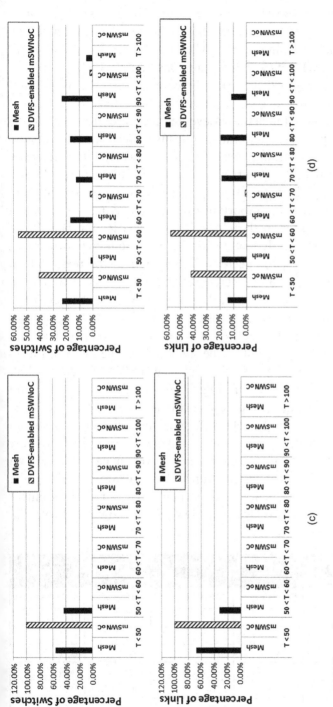

Figure 7.16 (Continued).

computational to moderately computational. The SPLASH-2 benchmarks are highly computational, and hence the communication among the cores is less than that in CANNEAL. Thus, network-level temperatures of the SPLASH-2 benchmarks are considerably lower than core temperatures. For these benchmarks, the cores govern the overall system temperature. As the degree of intercore communication increases, such as in CANNEAL, the network-level temperatures are comparable with the core temperatures. After a significantly high reduction in core temperature, by performing processor-level DVFS, the network becomes the bottleneck. After similarly performing network-level DVFS, we can keep the network temperature values in check as well. When the network plays an important role in the overall thermal characteristics of the chip, as in the CANNEAL scenario, the benefits of the mSWNoC can be clearly seen in Fig. 7.16d. The higher switch and link temperatures are greatly decreased compared to the mesh, which can be attributed to the large decrease in packet energy between the two architectures as seen in Fig. 7.11. From the switch characteristics seen in Fig. 7.16d, the mesh architecture has switch temperatures exceeding 100°C, while the mSWNoC does not. Similarly, the link characteristics in Fig. 7.16d follow the same trend. The mesh has links that have temperatures above 90°C, while the mSWNoC reduces link temperatures to below 60°C. In Fig. 7.16a−c, the FFT, LU, and RADIX traffic types fall on the other extreme for network-level thermal characteristics due to the relatively more intensive computational nature of the benchmarks. As the entire network is below 70°C in these scenarios, thermal concerns are limited; however, it can still be seen that the mesh shows higher temperatures. As an example, ΔT_{avg}, the average temperature reduction per switch and per link segment between the mesh and mSWNoC with DVFS are shown in Table 7.5.

Table 7.5 Change in Network Temperatures Between Non-DVFS Mesh and Dual-Level DVFS mSWNoC		FFT (°C)	RADIX (°C)	LU (°C)	CANNEAL (°C)
Switch	ΔT_{avg}	6.09	3.24	3.47	21.60
	ΔT_{max}	15.33	7.59	8.79	25.32
	$\Delta T_{hotspot}$	13.74	6.78	7.68	25.32
Link	ΔT_{avg}	5.13	2.74	2.92	18.24
	ΔT_{max}	10.09	6.21	5.76	35.93
	$\Delta T_{hotspot}$	9.96	6.14	5.67	31.64

Similar to the cores, we also show the values of $\Delta T_{\text{hotspot}}$ and ΔT_{max} for the switches and links in Table 7.5 as well. From the sharp increase in temperature savings for the network running CANNEAL traffic, it can be noted that as traffic intensity increases, there is more room for thermal savings within the network. In the highest temperature scenario (CANNEAL), the temperatures of the hottest switch and the hottest link in a mesh architecture have been reduced by 25.32°C and 35.93°C, respectively, in the DVFS-enabled mSWNoC, while the hotspot temperatures have been reduced by 25.32°C and 31.64°C, among the switches and links, respectively, which is a direct result in the drastic energy reductions displayed in Fig. 7.11.

REFERENCES

Bienia, C., 2011. Benchmarking modern multiprocessors (Ph.D. dissertation). Department of Computer Science, Princeton University, Princeton NJ.

Binkert, N., Beckmann, B., Black, G., Reinhardt, S.K., Saidi, A., Basu, A., et al., 2011. The GEM5 simulator. ACM SIGARCH Comput. Archit. News 39 (2), 1–7.

Deb, S., Chang, K., Yu, X., Sah, S.P., Cosic, M., Ganguly, A., et al., 2012. Design of an energy efficient CMOS compatible NoC architecture with millimeter-wave wireless interconnects. IEEE Trans. Comput 62, 2382–2396.

Kim, W., Gupta, M., Wei, G.-Y., Brooks, D., 2008. System level analysis of fast, per-core dvfs using on-chip switching regulators. In: Proceedings of the International Symposium on High Performance Computer Architecture. pp. 123–134.

Kudva, S.S., Harjani, R., 2011. Fully-integrated on-chip DC-DC converter with a 450X output range. IEEE J. Solid-State Circuits 46 (8), 1940–1951.

Lee, J., Nam, B., Yoo, H., Dynamic voltage and frequency scaling (DVFS) scheme for multi-domains power management. In: IEEE Asian Solid-State Circuits Conference (ASSCC '07), November 2007. pp. 360–363.

Li, S., Ahn, J.H., Strong, R., Brockman, J., Tullsen, D., Jouppi, N., 2009. McPAT: an integrated power, area, and timing modeling framework for multicore and manycore architectures. In: Proceedings of the International Symposium on Microarchitecture. pp. 469–480.

Sankaranarayanan, K., Velusamy, S., Stan, M., Skadron, K., 2005. A case for thermal-aware floorplanning at the microarchitectural level. J. Instruct. Level Parallel. 7, 1–16.

Shang, L., Peh, L.-S., Jha, N., 2002. Power-efficient interconnection networks: dynamic voltage scaling with links. Comput. Archit. Lett. 1, 6.

Skadron, K., et al., 2003. Temperature-aware microarchitecture. In: Proceedings of the International Symposium on Computer Architecture. pp. 2–13.

Usman, S., Khan, S.U., Khan, S., 2013. A comparative study of voltage/frequency scaling in NoC. In: IEEE International Conference on Electro/Information Technology (EIT), May 9–11, 2013. pp. 1–5.

Woo, S.C., Ohara, M., Torrie, E., Singh, J.P., Gupta, A., 1995. The SPLASH-2 programs: characterization and methodological considerations. In: Proceedings of ISCA. pp. 24–36.

CHAPTER 8

Dynamic Thermal Management

From Chapter 7, and more specifically Fig. 7.14, it is evident that performing DVFS at both the core and network alone does not address all concerns regarding temperature variations on the NoC. However, these relative temporal and spatial hotspots can be addressed through several DTM techniques. This chapter describes the DTM techniques performed on both processing cores and network elements for the mSWNoC architecture. The specific core-level DTM is a temperature-aware task allocation heuristic, while the network-level DTM principally involves a temperature-aware adaptive routing strategy. The selections of DTM strategies in this chapter are examples of DTM for the mSWNoC architecture, and this architecture is not bound to the specific strategies discussed in this chapter.

TEMPERATURE-AWARE TASK ALLOCATION

Uneven workloads and inefficient task allocations cause high-power densities in multicore chips resulting in temperature hotspots. Hence, thermal management techniques are explored to complement the benefits of the energy-efficient wireless NoC. The event-driven, thermal estimator proposed in Cui and Maskell (2012) is used for the temperature-aware task scheduling. The event-driven thermal estimator is based on power events. A power event is an increase or decrease in power dissipated by a core. The allocation or removal of a task from a core generates a power event with instantaneous power change at the beginning and end of the task.

A look-up table (LUT) approach, as described in Cui and Maskell (2012), is used as it is shown to be computationally less intensive compared to other existing models, while predicting the thermal profile of the chip very accurately. A LUT is used to model the thermal characteristics of the cores using a three-dimensional matrix consisting of multiple tables. Each table has the temperature trace of the chip when 1 W of power is injected into one particular core leaving the other cores untouched. Therefore, the number of tables is equal to the number of cores in the NoC. Each row in a particular table corresponds to the temperatures of all the cores at a particular instant of time. Hence, there are as many columns in each table as the number of cores. The number of samples required to reach the steady-state temperature across the chip determines the number of rows. To capture the transient thermal characteristics of the chip in response to unit power injection for each core separately, 2000 temperature samples were needed for every core to reach steady state. The number of samples required is determined by the chip size as larger chips require longer time to reach steady state. The LUT samples trace the temperature of all the cores requiring enough samples for the entire chip to reach steady state. Thus, the dimensions of the LUT are $N \cdot N \cdot 2000$ samples, where N is the number of cores on the chip. Considering each sample to be represented with single precision floating point numbers, for a system with 64 cores, the total amount of SRAM cells required is 31.25 MB. We envision that this LUT will be stored in the shared L2 cache. During the initialization phase of the chip, this LUT is used to perform the temperature-aware task allocation. Hence, no additional memory space is required for the LUT. Moreover, the LUT is used only once during the setup process, and hence its retrieval time does not affect the performance of the chip.

The future thermal map, T_{t_f}, at a future time, t_f, can be calculated based on the current thermal map, T_{t_c}, at current time, t_c, by adding the temperature increment of each core in the interval Δt to the current thermal map based on the power events as follows:

$$T_{t_f} = T_{t_c} + \Delta T_{\Delta t = t_f - t_c} \tag{8.1}$$

where T_{t_f}, T_{t_c}, and $\Delta T_{\Delta t = t_f - t_c}$ are N-element vectors denoting the future thermal maps, the current thermal map, and the temperature increment map of each of the N cores, respectively.

The temperature increment is calculated as follows:

$$\Delta T_{\Delta t = t_f - t_c} = \sum_{E_a \in E} P_{E_a} \times \left(LUT_{row_{t_f}} - LUT_{row_{t_c}} \right)_{Core_{E_a}} \tag{8.2}$$

where E_a is an atomic power event in the list of events E and P_{E_a} is the power associated with that event. LUT_{row} denotes a row of the LUT for time t_f and t_c, respectively, for the LUT of core given by $Core_{E_a}$, the core where the power event occurs.

The Future Temperature Trends (FTT) heuristic (Cui and Maskell, 2012) is used to obtain a temperature-aware task allocation as it generates task allocations with lowest peak and average temperatures. The FTT heuristic classifies all the idle cores into two sets, namely, $Core_+$, for cores with increasing temperature, and $Core_-$, for cores with decreasing temperature, based on the difference in current and predicted temperature for that core. Following this, each core is assigned a weight, T_w, as:

$$T_w = \begin{cases} T \times a_+ & \text{if } core \in Core_+ \\ T/a_- & \text{if } core \in Core_- \end{cases} \tag{8.3}$$

where T is the current core temperature, a_+ is the temperature increment, and a_- is the temperature decrement. Allocating a queued task sorted in descending order according to power, to the core with minimum weight, is shown to have thermally optimal results (Cui and Maskell, 2012). However, the performance resulting from this allocation may not be optimal. In order to obtain the optimal performance, the task allocation heuristic is modified to take into consideration the characteristics of the NoC. The weights assigned to the cores obtained from (8.3) are combined with another weight parameter, P_W, which captures the performance of the NoC. For any available core, this weight is the average distance between the tasks that are already allocated, when the next queued task is mapped to that core. For each available core i, this weight is calculated as follows:

$$P_w = \sum_{j \in Alloc\_Set} h_{ij} \cdot f_{ij} \quad i = \text{current core} \tag{8.4}$$

where $Alloc\_Set$ is the set of all tasks that are already allocated on the NoC, h_{ij} is the distance in number of hops between core i and the core where task j is allocated, and f_{ij} is the frequency of communication between the queued task mapped on core i and task j. The weights obtained from (8.3) and (8.4) are normalized and combined to calculate a final weight as follows:

$$W = \phi \hat{T}_w + (1 - \phi) \hat{P}_w \tag{8.5}$$

where $\hat{T}_w$ is the set of normalized thermal weights with respect to the maximum, $\hat{P}_w$ is the set of normalized performance weights with respect to the maximum, and ϕ is a weight parameter between 0 and 1 that controls the importance of either performance or temperature on the task allocation heuristic. The core for task allocation is selected as the one with minimum W, obtained from (8.5). This thermal management scheme is used for reallocating the tasks on cores for optimization of the thermal profile as well as the performance.

TEMPERATURE-AWARE ADAPTIVE ROUTING

In the mSWNoC architecture, specific switches tend to attract high levels of traffic (Wettin et al., 2013). This problem is further aggravated when those switches are generating or receiving high volumes of traffic, due to the nature of the specific benchmarks under consideration. Specific traffic patterns, some of which are heavily imbalanced, may cause thermal hotspots among the network components. Hence, traffic not destined for the hotspot switch should attempt to avoid it. The temperature-aware adaptive routing scheme proposed in this work was developed to (1) monitor and (2) avoid forming local hotspots.

As temperature is closely related to the energy dissipation of the chip, the thermal profile of the NoC depends on the energy dissipation of the network elements. To obtain the thermal profiles of a particular part of the network the average communication density is utilized as the relevant parameter. The average communication density is defined by (8.6):

$$\rho_{\text{comm}_i} = \frac{N_{f_i}}{W_S} \qquad (8.6)$$

where ρ_{comm_i} is the communication density for switch i expressed in flits per cycle (FPC), W_S is the monitoring window size in cycles, and N_{f_i} is the number of flits handled by switch i in the monitoring window. This is similar to (7.8), however, in this case is computed at a per switch level. The higher the communication density a switch has, the more power it dissipates in the given window. When the switch power increases, the temperature increases. Hence, the communication density of the switch can be used to monitor its thermal behavior. Similarly, link communication density can also be defined in the same regard, as the number of FPC that are transmitted on a given link.

After all switch communication densities have been determined, a method to avoid hotspot switches was developed. First, a threshold, β, was set in order to detect which switches have relatively high communication densities. If the communication density of a switch exceeds β by the end of a given monitoring window, that switch is put on an avoidance list. If a switch's communication density continuously exceeds β, it is avoided exponentially to the number of times β is exceeded in a row.

When a message is generated in the network, the path with the smallest distance to the destination should be taken to minimize latency and maximize throughput. However, if that path contains switches with communication densities higher than the above-mentioned parameter β, that path should only be taken with a certain probability. By attempting to avoid a path with a hotspot switch, we minimize the amount of traffic that the hotspot switch may handle, however we do not completely block the path to all traffic. As the approach is dynamically aware of relative-hotspot situations, extreme measures for reducing temperature are unnecessary. The probability of following any path is determined by the path ratio, R_{path}, given in (8.7):

$$R_{\text{path}} = \begin{cases} 1, & \text{unthrottled path} \\ \dfrac{1}{L} \prod_{i \in \text{path}} r_i, & \text{otherwise} \end{cases} \qquad (8.7)$$

where an unthrottled path (a path with no switches on the avoidance list) has a path ratio of 1, and a throttled path has a path ratio defined above. Here, L is the path length, and r_i is i_{th} switch's throttling ratio, defined in (8.8):

$$r_i = \left(\frac{1}{NT_i + 1} \right)^{NT_i} \qquad (8.8)$$

In (8.8), NT_i is the number of consecutive throttle attempts for a given switch (the number of times the switch has been on the avoidance list consecutively). As can be seen in (8.8), the longer a switch remains on the avoidance list, it is avoided with a larger probability.

For a particular source–destination pair, a list of ranked paths is considered. R_n, the nth ranked path ratio, is determined starting with the lowest ranked path and continuing until an unthrottled path is found; or all of the paths have been checked. The ranked paths are then compared probabilistically in order to determine which path will be selected for routing. The flow of the temperature-aware adaptive algorithm, which was explained earlier, is shown in Fig. 8.1.

For the mesh architecture, a temperature-aware adaptive routing scheme is developed similar to Shang et al. (2006), where data belonging

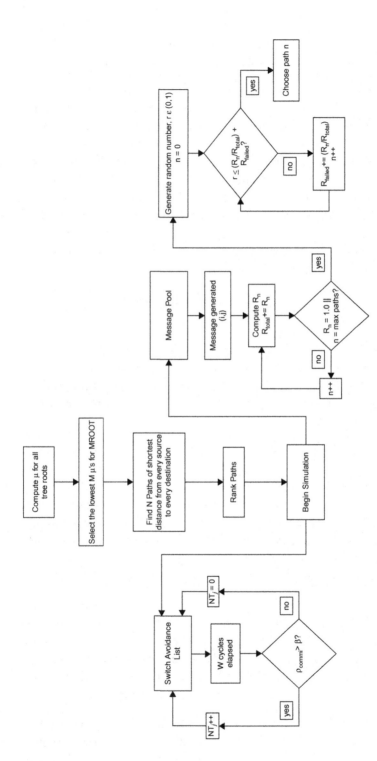

Figure 8.1 Temperature-aware rerouting algorithm flowchart.

to all except one virtual channel follow a regular $X-Y$ routing strategy. If a switch exceeds the threshold β, it uses the hotspot avoidance methodology described earlier in this section. When a packet is injected into the network, if its $X-Y$ route would pass through a thermally congested switch, it is placed on the last virtual channel that is used for rerouting.

For both the mSWNoC and mesh architectures, when a packet has been chosen to be rerouted, its rerouted path is computed from the source, in full, to the destination. This path is ensured to be deadlock free as it follows the same MROOTS-based routing scheme. The only potential disruption to this chosen path is due to the inaccessibility of a wireless channel. Dynamic Quick Reconfiguration (DQR), as presented in Sem-Jacobsen and Lysne (2012), is used to ensure deadlock freedom. In this situation, the current WI becomes the new source for the packet, which then takes a wireline only path to the final destination, still following the original up/down routing restrictions.

EXPERIMENTAL RESULTS

In this section, the performance and temperature profile of the mSWNoC is evaluated and compared with the conventional mesh-based NoC. We further evaluate the influence of both the processor- and network-level DTM elaborated in earlier sections of this chapter on both architectures as well. The experimental platform remains unchanged from earlier chapters.

Root Node Selection for MROOTS

As discussed in Chapter 5, the number and placement of roots for MROOTS-based routing can affect the performance of the mSWNoC architecture. Fig. 8.2 shows the variation of latency with respect to the location of the roots for the various traffics. As the mSWNoC architecture has four virtual channels, the number of trees, and hence roots, is also four (Lysne et al., 2006). Performance of the mSWNoC in the presence of the three tree root selection policies as described in Chapter 5 was evaluated. It can be seen that the traffic-weighted minimized hop-count placement (f_{ij}) obtains the optimum performance (least latency) for the mSWNoC architecture. Hence, this root selection strategy is used for the following performance evaluation.

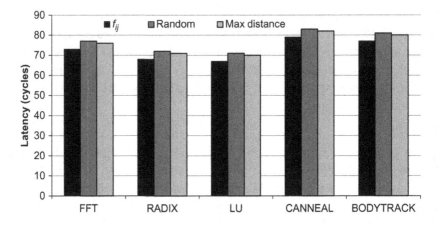

Figure 8.2 Packet latency for mSWNoC with different root placement strategies.

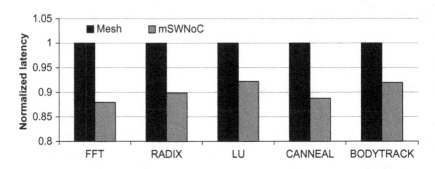

Figure 8.3 Average normalized network latency with various traffic patterns.

mSWNoC Performance Evaluation

In this section, first the latency and network-level energy dissipation characteristics are presented of the mSWNoC- and mesh-based wireline NoC architectures. Further comparisons are made for the temperature characteristics of the two architectures.

Latency and Energy Characteristics

Figs. 8.3 and 8.4 show the latency and network energy for the mSWNoC and mesh, respectively, considering the FFT, RADIX, LU, CANNEAL, and BODYTRACK. It can be observed from Fig. 8.3 that for all of the benchmarks considered, the latency of mSWNoC is lower than that of the mesh architecture. This is due to the small-world network-based interconnect infrastructure of mSWNoC with direct long-range wireless links that enables a smaller average hop

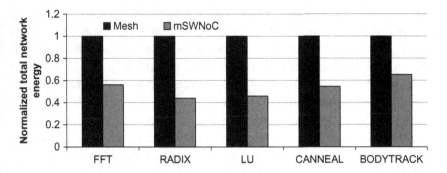

Figure 8.4 Normalized total network energy with various traffic patterns.

count than that of mesh (Ganguly et al., 2011). Due to the connectivity of the small-world architecture, the average network latency is reduced by 12.1%, 10.1%, 7.8%, 11.2%, and 8.0% for FFT, RADIX, LU, CANNEAL, and BODYTRACK, respectively. Also, it should be noted that the traffic injection load of these benchmarks is very low (Gratz and Keckler, 2010). Therefore, the networks operate much below the saturation point and for these injection loads, the possibility of latency improvements in mSWNoC is relatively small.

Fig. 8.4 shows the total network energy dissipation for both the mSWNoC and mesh architectures. We consider the total network energy dissipation to compare the characteristics of the two NoC architectures. It can be observed from Fig. 8.4 that in each benchmark, the network energy is much lower for the mSWNoC over the mesh architecture. There is a 43.9%, 56.2%, 54.3%, 45.4%, and 34.7% overall decrease in network energy between the mSWNoC and mesh architectures for FFT, RADIX, LU, CANNEAL, and BODYTRACK traffics, respectively. The two main contributors of the energy dissipation are from the switches and the interconnect infrastructure. In the mSWNoC, the overall switch energy decreases significantly compared to a mesh as a result of the better connectivity of the architecture. In this case, the hop count decreases significantly, and hence, on the average, packets have to traverse through less number of switches and links. In addition, a significant amount of traffic traverses through the energy-efficient wireless channels, consequently allowing the interconnect energy dissipation to decrease.

Network-Level Thermal Characteristics
In this section, the thermal profiles of the mesh- and mSWNoC-based architectures are evaluated. Initially, both architectures run the

benchmarks with a default random task allocation, which is chosen by the operating system. In this case, the random task placement on the cores is identical for both the architectures. Our aim here is to discuss the network-level temperature characteristics of mSWNoC and a regular mesh-based NoC architecture. To further understand architectural-based improvements in the thermal profile, we have obtained the average switch and link communication densities over the entire benchmark simulations. The average communication density, as defined in (7.8), was determined over the hotspot area of the network for each benchmark to analyze the thermal profile. Here, the hotspot area is defined as the original mesh location, which forms a localized region of high communication density and, hence, high temperatures.

The average wireline link communication densities in mSWNoC within the hotspot region of interest were reduced by 48.6%, 44.2%, 44.5%, 49.9%, and 51.3% for the FFT, RADIX, LU, CANNEAL, and BODYTRACK traffics, respectively, over the traditional mesh topology. The long-range wireless links significantly reduce the communication density of the hotspot region by efficiently carrying a major portion of the data, which would otherwise travel through the wireline links of the hotspot region. Similarly, savings of average switch communication densities were 47.8%, 45.1%, 41.6%, 54.9%, and 53.4% for the FFT, RADIX, LU, CANNEAL, and BODYTRACK traffics, respectively. This directly relates to the thermal profile of the chip, as reduction in communication density will produce less heat.

To demonstrate the thermal profile, we consider the CANNEAL benchmark as an example. It is one of the most communication-intensive benchmarks considered in this work as can be seen by the processor idle percentage time in Table 7.1. Hence, it is suitable to analyze the network-level temperature characteristics. As explained earlier, the HotSpot tool is used to determine the thermal profile of both architectures under consideration. To quantify the thermal improvements, the average reduction in switch or wireline link temperature between mesh and mSWNoC is defined as ΔT_{avg}, and the difference in maximum switch or link temperature between mesh and mSWNoC as $\Delta T_{hotspot}$. The average reduction in switch and link temperatures between mesh and mSWNoC are 23.12°C and 21.42°C, respectively, and $\Delta T_{hotspot}$ for the switches and links are 18.57°C and 27.18°C, respectively. As mentioned earlier, the improvement in network-level temperatures is due to the mSWNoC

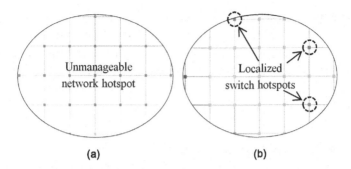

(a)   (b)

Figure 8.5 Network-induced hotspots in (a) Mesh and (b) mSWNoC.

having significantly lower communication density within the hotspot region of the respective mesh area.

The hotspots formed between the two architectures are quite different. In the mesh architecture, the network-induced hotspot is spread throughout a significant portion of the network, which can be seen in Fig. 8.5a. This also shows that both the switches and wireline links are causing the large network hotspot. The problem is somewhat unmanageable, as a majority of the network is becoming a thermal hotspot. The possibility of cooler alternate paths does not exist; hence, opportunity of any rerouting is limited. By introducing the mSWNoC architecture, there is still a network-induced hotspot. However, the hotspot switch temperature is 18.57°C lower than the mesh hotspot. In addition, by observing Fig. 8.5b, we can see that the problem is localized to specific switches, and does not concern the neighboring wireline links, which are much cooler. These switches are becoming traffic attractors, as they carry high traffic loads, through the long-range wireless and wireline links. Consequently, the network-induced hotspot scenario is certainly better in the mSWNoC compared to the mesh, where the thermal hotspot is spread over a large region of the network. Additionally, performing dynamic thermal management (DTM) among the cores can have significant effects on the overall temperature profile of the chip. However, temperature-aware task placement strategies leave the network vulnerable to become the new temperature bottleneck in the chip. For the mSWNoC architecture, a manageable network hotspot may form allowing the use of temperature-aware adaptive strategies efficiently. Both the effects of processor-level task migration and temperature-aware network rerouting will be evaluated in "Temperature-Aware Techniques" section.

Temperature-Aware Techniques

In this section, the required setup to implement the temperature-aware adaptive routing algorithm is discussed. Then the performance characteristics and thermal profile of the mSWNoC architecture by incorporating processor-level task placement and the temperature-aware rerouting mechanism are presented.

Temperature-Aware Adaptive Routing Setup

The temperature-aware adaptive routing algorithm requires tuning of the relevant parameters described earlier in order to optimize the achievable benefits. The two parameters that require tuning are the monitoring window size, W_S, and the throttling threshold, β, as described earlier. By varying W_S, we effectively define how fine-grained we want to monitor the incoming and outgoing traffic of the network switches. By varying β, we define how quickly we should begin to throttle potential future hotspot switches. For each benchmark, W_S and β are optimized in order to find the largest hotspot temperature reduction, or otherwise to maximize $\Delta T_{\text{hotspot}}$, between the mesh and temperature-aware mesh (tmesh) or mesh and temperature-aware mSWNoC (tmSWNoC) architectures. The temperature characteristics of a regular mesh-based NoC is considered the baseline here.

The window size varied between 100 and 1000 execution cycles, while β varied between $\rho_{\text{commavg}}/2$ and $2 \cdot \rho_{\text{commavg}}$, where ρ_{commavg} is the average switch communication density over the entire benchmark execution. We determined ρ_{commavg} experimentally for each benchmark prior to running the temperature-aware rerouting algorithm. The optimum configurations for the benchmarks considered in this work are presented in Table 8.1, which results in the largest hotspot temperature reduction as mentioned earlier.

Table 8.1 Optimized Rerouting Parameters				
	β		W_S	
	Mesh	mSWNoC	Mesh	mSWNoC
FFT	$\rho_{\text{commavg}}/2$	$\rho_{\text{commavg}}/2$	250	250
RADIX	$\rho_{\text{commavg}}/2$	$\rho_{\text{commavg}}/2$	250	100
LU	$\rho_{\text{commavg}}/2$	$\rho_{\text{commavg}}/2$	250	250
CANNEAL	$\rho_{\text{commavg}}/2$	ρ_{commavg}	250	100
BODYTRACK	$\rho_{\text{commavg}}/2$	ρ_{commavg}	250	100

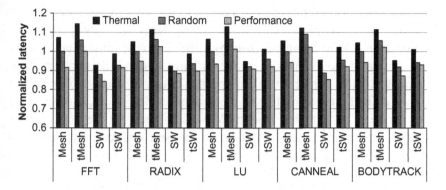

Figure 8.6 Normalized network packet latency of mesh and mSWNoC with and without DTM for various benchmarks.

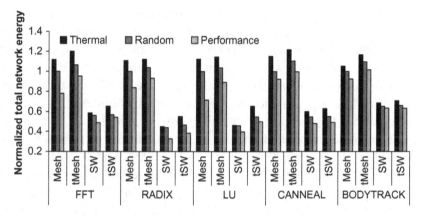

Figure 8.7 Normalized total network energy dissipation of mesh and mSWNoC with and without DTM for various benchmarks.

DTM Effects on Performance

Figs. 8.6 and 8.7 show the latency and network energy for the mSWNoC with various task placements, and with and without temperature-aware rerouting considering the five different benchmarks. These two parameters are also shown for the mesh-based NoC. It should be noted that the mesh and mSWNoC architectures with network-level DTM are labeled as tmesh and tmSWNoC, respectively. It can be observed from Fig. 8.6 that for each benchmark, when task placement is optimized for performance by setting ϕ to 0, the latency decreases with respect to the random task placement. This is due to the task placement minimizing the hop count as explained earlier. On the contrary, when thermal-aware task placement is used by setting ϕ to 1, the hop count is not minimized, leading to a higher average latency. In addition to task placement, it is clearly seen that by performing temperature-aware adaptive routing, the inherent improvements to latency due to the mSWNoC architecture are lessened. By choosing less-efficient paths in order to avoid specific hotspots, certain packets are taking paths that may not have the minimum hop count. However, as can be seen in Fig. 8.6, the mSWNoC latency in the presence of temperature-aware adaptive routing for the benchmarks under consideration is still less than the latency in the mesh architecture.

It can be observed from Fig. 8.7 that in each benchmark the network energy is lower when the task placement is optimized for performance. This is again due to tasks being placed to minimize hop count. Also, the benefits of the hop-count minimization are greater in the mSWNoC as it takes the most advantage of performance-aware task placement. As shown in Fig. 8.7, there is a slight increase in total network energy between the mSWNoC and temperature-aware mSWNoC. As explained in the prior paragraph, as nonoptimum paths can be taken, the number of stages that certain packets may take will increase. This in turn causes the network energy to increase. From Fig. 8.7, however, it can be observed that the increase in overall energy is quite small. In fact, for the benchmarks considered, there is an increase in energy from the original mSWNoC by only 0.7%, 2.6%, 8.9%, 0.5%, and 0.7% for FFT, RADIX, LU, CANNEAL, and BODYTRACK, respectively, for randomly placed tasks. Even after incorporating temperature-aware adaptive routing, the mSWNoC still dissipates significantly less energy than a conventional wireline mesh.

It should be noted that the addition of various task placements and the temperature-aware adaptive routing algorithms do not have noticeable negative impacts on the mSWNoC performance. However, the improvements of the thermal profile of the mSWNoC-enabled multicore architectures will be demonstrated in Temperature Analysis of Task Allocation, and Avoiding Local Hotspots sections.

Temperature Analysis of Task Allocation
In Fig. 8.8, we present the average and maximum core temperatures by incorporating various DTM techniques on both mesh and mSWNoC architectures. Here, it can be seen that temperature-aware task placement allows the temperature among the cores to decrease. This is

(a)

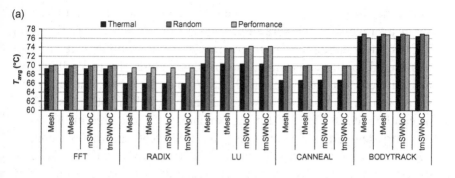

(b)

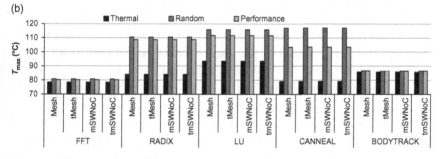

Figure 8.8 (a) Average and (b) maximum core temperatures.

evident from Fig. 8.8 and shown by a decrease in average and maximum core temperatures among the benchmarks.

As both these parameters are decreasing, the temperature of the hottest core with random task allocation is being reduced (removing the original hotspot), and the new maximum core temperature is also less. In the FFT and BODYTRACK benchmarks, the change in hotspot temperature is small because the tasks within those benchmarks are evenly distributed. RADIX, LU, and CANNEAL have much higher opportunities for hotspot temperature savings as those benchmarks are less evenly distributed. Here, the workload is dominated by a few tasks, and hence the power and temperature for the cores running those tasks are high. By adopting temperature-aware task allocation, where cores running highly active tasks are placed toward the chip edge, closest to the heat sink, a large reduction in temperature is achieved. As an example, in the case of the CANNEAL benchmark the random task placements create core temperatures as high as 117.1°C. The temperature-aware allocation produces a hottest core temperature of 79.19°C avoiding thermal emergencies (Sankaranarayanan et al., 2005).

In the presence of performance-aware task placement, there is a slight average core temperature increase from the random allocation. This is understandable due to the fact that core temperatures are not considered for task placement in this case. Here, the task allocations are different between mesh and mSWNoC. However, the tasks dissipate similar amounts of power irrespective of their locations. Hence, as can be seen in Fig. 8.8, for the benchmarks considered in this work, the core temperatures for mesh and mSWNoC in the presence of performance-aware task allocation are also nearly identical. The main difference will be observed in the temperature profiles of the NoC switches and links.

The thermal characteristics of the network are shown in Fig. 8.9. As mentioned in Table 7.1, the chosen benchmarks vary from highly computational to moderately computational. The SPLASH-2 benchmarks considered in this work are highly computational, and hence the communication among the cores is less than that in CANNEAL and BODYTRACK. Thus, network-level temperatures of the SPLASH-2 benchmarks are considerably lower than core temperatures. For these benchmarks, the cores govern the overall system temperature. As the degree of intercore communication increases, such as in CANNEAL, the network-level temperatures are comparable with the core temperatures. In BODYTRACK, the network temperatures have surpassed the core temperatures. In CANNEAL, after a significantly high reduction in core temperature, by performing temperature-aware task placement, the network becomes the temperature bottleneck. Here, the difference between architectures becomes noticeable. When the network plays an important role in the overall thermal characteristics of the chip, as in the CANNEAL and BODYTRACK scenarios, the benefits of the mSWNoC can be clearly seen in Fig. 8.9. The higher switch and link temperatures are greatly decreased compared to mesh, which can be attributed to the decrease in overall network energy between the two architectures as seen in Fig. 8.7.

Avoiding Local Hotspots
As previously mentioned, the goal of this chapter was to minimize the impact on mSWNoC performance while improving the overall thermal profile by reducing the temperature of hotspot areas. Once again, we will consider the CANNEAL and BODYTRACK benchmarks as they are the most communication-intensive applications, as

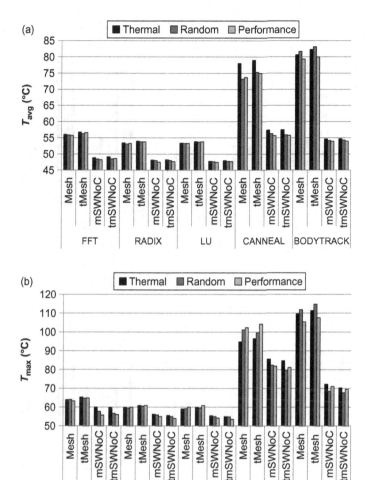

Figure 8.9 (a) Average and (b) maximum switch temperatures. (c) Average and (d) maximum wireline link temperatures.

seen in Table 7.1. Hence, the effects of temperature-aware adaptive routing on the network thermal characteristics can be clearly seen. Here, we can see the distinct advantages of the temperature-aware adaptive routing algorithm. In both CANNEAL and BODYTRACK there is an interesting relationship between rerouting on the mesh and rerouting on the mSWNoC architectures. As mentioned earlier, and seen in Fig. 8.5, the widespread hotspot of mesh may not be helped through rerouting. This, in fact, holds true. As can be seen in Table 8.2, after performing temperature-aware rerouting in the

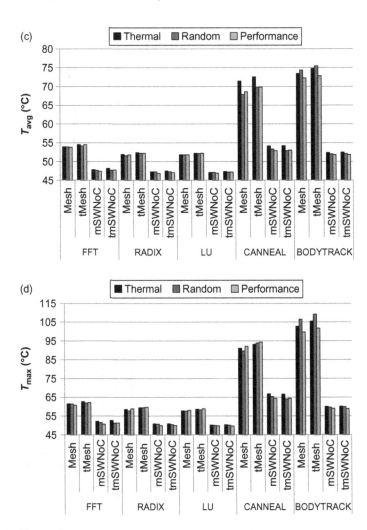

Figure 8.9 (Continued).

unmanageable hotspot region, the average switch and link temperatures have increased by 1.53°C and 1.35°C, respectively, for CANNEAL, and 1.79°C and 1.35°C, respectively, for BODYTRACK. The maximum switch and link temperatures have also increased, as can be seen in Table 8.2. However, the original hotspot temperature has in fact been reduced by 2.15°C in CANNEAL. This was the intent of performing rerouting on the mesh. While reducing the hotspot, a new switch has surpassed the original hotspot switch temperature. While the goal was to decrease the hotspot by routing away from the problem area, the

Table 8.2 Hotspot Growth in Mesh and Shrink in mSWNoC Architectures After Performing Network-Level Rerouting

Benchmark		Hotspot Increase (%)		T_{avg} Increase (°C)		T_{max} Increase (°C)	
		Mesh	mSWNoC	Mesh	mSWNoC	Mesh	mSWNoC
CANNEAL	Switch	3.70	0	1.52	−1.51	1.71	−0.76
	Link	7.14	4.17	1.35	−0.08	2.05	0.20
BODYTRACK	Switch	9.09	0	1.79	−1.06	1.70	−1.89
	Link	10.253	3.13	1.35	−0.01	2.90	0.01

mesh rerouting has in fact resulted in the opposite effect. In this case, the hotspot temperatures have increased, and have made the overall hotspot larger. A larger hotspot, in this sense means that more switches and links have increased to a temperature beyond the third quartile of the original chip temperature spread, and are now considered part of the hotspot area. This is due to the large area hotspot seen in Fig. 8.5a, as there is no effective alternate path that will not end up creating more traffic in the hotspot area. On the other hand, we can also see how the average switch and link temperatures in the hotspot have decreased for the mSWNoC architecture. The average switch and link hotspot temperatures have decreased by 1.51°C and 0.08°C, respectively, for CANNEAL, and 1.06°C and 0.01°C, respectively, for BODYTRACK on the mSWNoC architecture. Additionally the maximum switch hotspot temperatures have decreased by 0.76°C and 1.89°C, respectively, for CANNEAL and BODYTRACK. The maximum link hotspot temperatures have slightly increased by 0.20°C and 0.01°C for the mSWNoC architecture. This can be expected as we have chosen a potentially longer route in order to decrease the hotspot switch. In the mSWNoC scenario with CANNEAL traffic placed using thermal-task placement, the maximum chip temperature with adaptive routing was reduced to a maximum of 84.79°C (Fig. 8.9b), creating a much more sustainable temperature compared to the staggering 117.1°C (Fig. 8.8b) from the original mesh architecture without rerouting and with random task placement.

REFERENCES

Cui, J., Maskell, D., 2012. A fast high-level event-driven thermal estimator for dynamic thermal aware scheduling. IEEE Trans. Comput. Aided Design Integr. Circuits Syst. 31 (6).

Ganguly, A., Wettin, P., Chang, K., Pande, P.P., 2011. Complex network inspired fault-tolerant NoC architectures with wireless links. In: Proc. of ACM/IEEE NOC Symposium.

Gratz, P., Keckler, S., 2010.Realistic workload characterization and analysis for Networks-on-Chip design. In: The 4th Workshop on Chip Multiprocessor Memory Systems and Interconnects (CMP-MSI).

Lysne, O., Skeie, T., Reinemo, S.-A., Theiss, I., 2006. Layered routing in irregular networks. IEEE Trans. Parallel Distrib. Syst. 17 (1), 51–65.

Sankaranarayanan, K., Velusamy, S., Stan, M., Skadron, K., 2005. A case for thermal-aware floorplanning at the microarchitectural level. J. Instruct. Level Parallel. 1–16.

Sem-Jacobsen, F.O., Lysne, O., 2012. Topology agnostic dynamic quick reconfiguration for large-scale interconnection networks. In: IEEE/ACM International Symposium on Cluster, Cloud and Grid Computing, pp. 228–235.

Shang, L., Peh, L.-S., Jha, N.K., 2006. PowerHerd: a distributed scheme for dynamically satisfying peak-power constraints in interconnection networks. IEEE Trans. Comput. Aided Design Integr. Circuits Syst. 25 (1), 92–110.

Wettin, P., Murray, J., Pande, P.P., Shirazi, B., Ganguly, A., 2013. Energy-efficient multicore chip design through cross-layer approach. In: Proc. of IEEE Design, Automation, & Test in Europe (DATE).

CHAPTER 9

Joint DTM and DVFS Techniques

ENHANCED ROUTING AND DYNAMIC THERMAL MANAGEMENT

In Chapters 7 and 8, dynamic voltage and frequency scaling (DVFS) and dynamic thermal management (DTM) techniques for the millimeter-wave SWNoC (mSWNoC) architecture were proposed as separate entities. In this chapter, a joint application of network-level DTM and DVFS techniques for the mSWNoC architecture is introduced. The power law connectivity-based mSWNoC principally has an irregular network topology. Routing in irregular networks is more complex, because the routing methods need to be topology agnostic. Hence, it is necessary to investigate suitable routing mechanisms for mSWNoCs to ensure deadlock-free routing. Irregular networks can have routing strategies that are either rule- or path-driven (Flich et al., 2012). For comparison, routing strategies from both categories have been adopted.

ALASH-Based Routing

The first routing strategy is an adaptive layered shortest path (ALASH) routing algorithm (Flich et al., 2012), which belongs to the path-based classification which is detailed in Chapter 5.

For ALASH, the decision to switch paths is based on current network conditions, such as virtual channel availability and current communication density of the network. To estimate the congestion of a particular part of the network we propose to utilize the average communication density, ρ_{comm}, as the relevant parameter, which is defined by (7.8) in Chapter 7. The higher ρ_{comm} a switch has the more power it dissipates in the given window. When the switch energy increases, the temperature increases. Hence, the ρ_{comm} of the switch can be used to monitor its thermal behavior. Therefore, at every switch in the path, ALASH makes an evaluation regarding which link to follow based on ρ_{comm} in order to reduce congestion in the network. This is done by choosing the path j that minimizes ρ_{path} given in (9.1)

$$\rho_{\text{path}} = \sum_{i=1}^{\text{pathlength}(j)} \rho_{\text{comm}_{\text{path}(j,i)}} \tag{9.1}$$

where path(j,i) represents the ith link of the jth path, ρ_{comm} is the communication density defined in (7.8) and pathlength(j) is the number of links in the path j. Since ALASH always takes the shortest physical path, this type of adaptive routing does not add extra hops to the path. As ρ_{comm} is used to determine the suitable paths for the data packets, this helps to evenly distribute the traffic and reduce congestion in the network. By balancing the load across the network, this type of routing is inherently beneficial to improve the thermal profile of the mSWNoC.

Adaptive MROOTS-Based Routing

To ensure deadlock-free routing in the second routing strategy, we consider, belonging to the rule-based classification, the MROOTS-based mechanism defined in Chapter 5. A congestion-aware adaptive routing strategy was built upon MROOTS (AMROOTS) following the congestion detection and recovery methodology. As MROOTS does not guarantee shortest path, using the ALASH-based congestion-aware technique would only produce longer routing paths. Hence, we implement the congestion detection and recovery method, described shortly in further detail on MROOTS to make AMROOTS.

JOINT DTM/DVFS

The small-world architectures discussed in Chapter 4 and the congestion-aware routing schemes discussed in Chapter 5, modify the distribution of network traffic patterns significantly. Hence, it is possible to tune the voltage and frequency of the small-world switches and links depending on the traffic-dependent bandwidth requirements.

First, by reducing the hop count between largely separated communicating cores, wireless shortcuts have been shown to carry a significant amount of the overall traffic within an mSWNoC (Wettin et al., 2013). The amount of traffic detoured in this way is substantial and the low-power wireless links enable energy savings. However, as previously discussed, the energy dissipation within the network is still dominated by the data traversing the wireline links. Hence, the overall energy dissipation of the mSWNoC can be improved even further if the characteristics of the wireline links are optimized. Consequently, implementing DVFS on the wireline links and the associated switch ports of an mSWNoC-enabled multicore architecture has the potential for more energy savings. Second, as discussed earlier in this book, ALASH and AMROOTS inherently reduce traffic relayed through relative hotspot switches. Attempting to evenly distribute traffic among the network elements to reduce congestion does this for ALASH. In AMROOTS, by explicitly routing away from relative hotspot switches, the amount of traffic on these switches will be significantly reduced. As traffic that is not created nor destined for the given hotspot switch will avoid it, if possible, the utilization of links associated with the hotspot switch will be lowered, provided that the switch remains on the avoidance list. Hence, in this chapter, we propose two types of DVFS schemes where switches tune the voltages and frequencies of their corresponding ports and associated links depending on the nature of the traffic.

For ALASH, a DVFS strategy is used that combines both past (reactive) and future, (proactive) knowledge of the link utilizations to decide the voltage and frequency of the switch ports and associated links. For AMROOTS, a reactive DVFS strategy is first employed on nonhotspot switches, where the ports and links are tuned according to their utilizations. Then, a proactive DVFS strategy is employed where knowledge of the network, such as hotspot switches and communication densities, are used to estimate its impact on other sections of the network and tune the ports and links accordingly. Hence, every switch can utilize proactive and/or reactive DVFS given its traffic-dependent, relative hotspot characteristics.

Reactive DVFS

A method for history-based DVFS for the mSWNoC was proposed in Chapter 7. This type of DVFS is used as the base DVFS algorithm for both the ALASH- and AMROOTS-based mechanisms. To reiterate from Chapter 7, every NoC switch predicts future traffic patterns based on an exponential weighted average history determined for each link. The short-term link utilization is characterized by

$$U_{\text{short}} = \frac{1}{H} \sum_{i=1}^{H} b_i \qquad (9.2)$$

where H is the prediction window, and b_i is 1 if a flit traversed the link on the ith cycle of the history window, and 0 otherwise. The predicted future link utilization, $U_{\text{Predicted}}$, is an exponential weighted average determined for each link according to

$$U_{\text{Predicted}} = \frac{W * U_{\text{short}} + U_{\text{Predicted}}(t-1)}{W+1} \tag{9.3}$$

where $U_{\text{Predicted}}(t-1)$ is $U_{\text{Predicted}}$ for the previous DVFS window and W is the weight between the current history window and the previous windows. As mentioned earlier, we propose to combine this history-based prediction with the ALASH and AMROOTS routing decisions, respectively, to implement the overall DVFS mechanism.

Proactive DVFS
As the basic path selection method depends on the exact routing methodology, the exact proactive DVFS implementation varies between ALASH and AMROOTS.

In ALASH, at any particular time, every switch knows which link a message is going to take to reach a particular destination. This information can be used to predict the future link utilizations for the links connected to the switch. If there are not many messages destined for a particular link according to the ALASH decision-making mechanism, then the utilization for that link in the near-future can be predicted to be low. This prediction, $U_{\text{Proactive}}$, is defined below

$$U_{\text{Proactive}} = \sum_{j=0}^{N} \left[D(j) * \sum_{i=1}^{H} B_i(j) \right] \tag{9.4}$$

where N is the number of switches in the network, $B_i(j)$ is 1 if a flit destined for switch j traversed the link on the ith cycle of the history window and 0 otherwise, and $D(j)$ is 1 if the next flit destined for switch j will use the link and 0 otherwise. $U_{\text{Proactive}}$ from (9.4) is used with $U_{\text{Predicted}}$ from (9.3), to create a new prediction, U_{ALASH}, defined as

$$U_{\text{ALASH}} = \sigma * U_{\text{Predicted}} + \gamma * U_{\text{Proactive}} \tag{9.5}$$

where σ and γ are weight parameters, for $U_{\text{Predicted}}$ and $U_{\text{Proactive}}$, respectively, that are optimized for a certain latency performance requirement point which will be described in the experimental results. Using (9.5), we are able to control how much DVFS relies on the history, using weight σ, and on the future routing, using weight γ.

As the AMROOTS routing strategy is implemented on the mSWNoC architecture, there is some inherent knowledge in the avoidance list, which can be useful for tuning the voltages and frequencies of the various switch ports and associated links. When a switch is added to the avoidance list, utilization will be heavily reduced, as traffic will try to avoid routing through the hotspot. Hence, a method for performing proactive DVFS was adopted. The proactive DVFS tunes the voltage/frequency (V/F) of a given hotspot switches' ports and associated links down when the switch is on the avoidance list. As our first priority is to reduce switch temperature hotspots as much as possible, proactive DVFS combined with the adaptive routing strategy is important to help reduce the affected hotspot quickly. This is done by not only mitigating much of the through-switch traffic but also reducing the V/F of the affected switches' ports and links to allow it to cool down faster. This DVFS methodology is also implemented on the mesh architecture for undertaking a detailed comparative evaluation.

EXPERIMENTAL RESULTS

In this section, we evaluate the performance and temperature profiles of the mSWNoC and SWNoC (small-world NoC without wireless shortcuts), using the ALASH and AMROOTS routing and DVFS strategies elaborated earlier in the chapter. For an exhaustive comparison, we also consider the performance and temperature profile of the conventional wireline mesh. The architecture of SWNoC is the same as that of the mSWNoC with long-range wired links instead of wireless shortcuts. Each switch port has four virtual channels. Hence, four trees are created for AMROOTS and four layers are created for ALASH. In this chapter, and defined in Table 7.3, we consider nominal range operation. Hence, the adopted DVFS strategy uses discrete V/F pairs that maintain a linear relationship. The considered levels are: 1 V/2.5 GHz, 0.9 V/2.25 GHz, 0.8 V/2.0 GHz, 0.7 V/1.75 GHz, 0.6 V/1.5 GHz, and 0.5 V/1.25 GHz. The experimental platform remains unchanged from earlier chapters.

DTM/DVFS Setup

The DTM methodology requires tuning of the relevant parameters described earlier in order to optimize the achievable benefits. For congestion-aware routing in ALASH and AMROOTS, the monitoring window size, W_S, requires tuning. By varying W_S, we effectively define how fine-grained we want to monitor the traffic of the network switches. For AMROOTS the parameter for throttling threshold, β, also needs to be tuned. By varying β, we define how quickly we should begin to throttle potential hotspot switches. For each benchmark, relevant parameters were optimized in order to find the largest hotspot temperature reduction between the mesh and congestion-aware ALASH and AMROOTS routing strategies on the mSWNoC.

In order to optimize the DVFS methodology, three parameters, the prediction window (how often $U_{\text{Predicted}}$ is updated), the proactive switching window (how often the V/F can change for proactive DVFS), and the reactive switching window (how often the V/F can change for reactive DVFS) were varied between 100 and 1200 execution cycles. A small reactive switching window may catch data bursts, which do not represent a long-term trend of the benchmark's traffic. Consequently, widely varying short-term traffic utilizations will cause the V/F to change often following the reactive DVFS. In this case, the regulator energy overhead may outweigh the benefits of a lower misprediction penalty. As both reactive and proactive windows widen, the regulator energy overhead impact is decreased, while the latency penalty increases. For ALASH, the two DVFS prediction parameters, σ and γ, were also optimized by individually varying the parameters to find the optimal configuration given a specific latency point. The case of increasing σ causes U_{ALASH} to follow $U_{\text{Predicted}}$ while increasing γ causes U_{ALASH} to follow $U_{\text{Proactive}}$ more closely. By increasing the sum of σ and γ a more conservative prediction for the upcoming window can be achieved, which results in a lower latency penalty but less energy savings, while decreasing the sum of σ and γ results in a more aggressive prediction with a higher latency penalty but more energy savings.

Performance Evaluation

In this section, we present the latency, energy dissipation, and thermal characteristics of the mSWNoC with ALASH and AMROOTS routing by incorporating the joint DTM and DVFS techniques described earlier. For completeness, we also show the characteristics of the conventional wireline mesh and the SWNoC architectures incorporating the joint DTM and DVFS techniques.

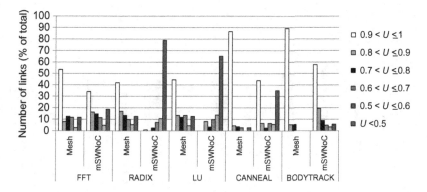

Figure 9.1 Link utilizations with various benchmarks.

DVFS Opportunities

The opportunity for performing DVFS on an NoC depends on the architecture's link utilization characteristics. A histogram of the link-level traffic utilizations is shown in Fig. 9.1. Here, we highlight the differences between the mesh and mSWNoC (with ALASH) to express the fact that the small-world architecture reduces link utilizations significantly. From this, it is seen that in the mesh architecture, a significant amount of links has more than 90% utilization for the considered benchmarks, and hence, the ability to perform link-level DVFS is low. In this case, there is not significant room for improvement with DVFS as the voltage and frequency cannot be tuned often on the links with high utilization without encountering excessive latency penalties. On the other hand, the mSWNoC reduces traffic on wireline links, which can also be seen clearly in Fig. 9.1. As the majority of links fall under 50% utilization in the mSWNoC architecture, there is significant opportunity for implementing DVFS. Because of this, there is room for more energy savings in mSWNoC in presence of DVFS compared to mesh. SWNoC also lowers link utilizations with respect to mesh. However, mSWNoC lowers it even further due to having wireless shortcuts. Also, differences between the routing strategies do not drastically affect these utilizations.

Latency and Energy Characteristics

Fig. 9.2 shows the latency for the various architectures and routing strategies. It can be observed from Fig. 9.2 that for all of the benchmarks considered, the latency of the small-world architectures with either routing strategies (ALASH and AMROOTS) are lower than that of the mesh architecture. This is due to the small-world

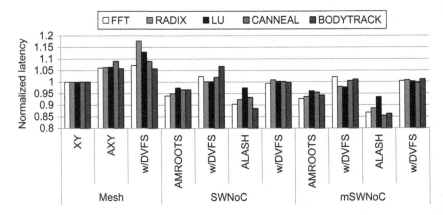

Figure 9.2 Normalized average network latency with various benchmarks.

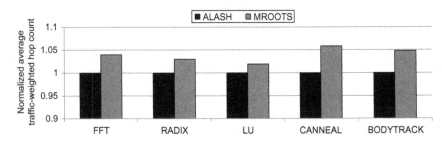

Figure 9.3 Normalized average traffic-weighted hop count between routing strategies for mSWNoC.

architecture of SWNoC and mSWNoC with direct long-range, one-hop wireline/wireless links that enables a smaller average hop count than that of mesh. Between the mSWNoC routing strategies, ALASH performs better for all the benchmarks considered. This is due to the fact that ALASH is able to route through the shortest physical path while AMROOTS has to route through the tree, which may require a greater amount of hops, and also has the potential for congestion at the root nodes. This is shown in Fig. 9.3, which displays a normalized average traffic-weighted hop count of the various benchmarks for the two routing strategies on the mSWNoC. Here it can be seen that the routing in ALASH takes fewer hops to reach destinations over the AMROOTS routing strategy. Also, as the path selection is chosen to minimize congestion, there is further room for ALASH to improve in latency over AMROOTS when message conflicts start to occur in the network. With the addition of DVFS, a performance target that matches the latency of the wireline mesh was selected. Hence, implementing DVFS

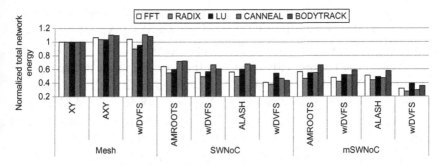

Figure 9.4 Normalized total network energy with various benchmarks.

on mSWNoC will not introduce a performance impact with respect to the mesh. It can also be seen that by implementing DTM and DVFS on the mesh architecture its respective latency increases due to V/F misprediction and nonoptimal path selection.

Fig. 9.4 shows the total network energy dissipation for the SWNoC, mSWNoC, and mesh architectures. It can be observed from Fig. 9.4 that in each benchmark, the network energy is much lower for the small-world architectures compared to the mesh architecture. The two main contributors of the energy dissipation are the switches and the interconnect infrastructure. In the small-world architectures, the overall switch energy decreases significantly compared to a mesh as a result of the better connectivity of these architectures. In this case, the hop count decreases significantly, and hence, on the average, packets have to traverse through less number of switches and links. In addition, a significant amount of traffic traverses through the energy-efficient wireless channels in mSWNoC, consequently allowing the interconnect energy dissipation of mSWNoC to further decrease compared to the SWNoC architecture. It can also be observed from Fig. 9.4 that the energy dissipation for ALASH and AMROOTS follows the same trend as that of the latency with ALASH having lower energy dissipation. When messages are in the network longer (higher latency), they dissipate more energy. The difference in energy dissipation arising out of the logic circuits of each individual routing is negligible and the overall energy dissipation is principally governed by the network characteristics.

With the addition of DVFS, the total network energy can be further reduced. As the traffic traversing through the wireline links is heavily reduced in the mSWNoC, the opportunity for implementing DVFS is significant. From Fig. 9.4, it is clear that for the CANNEAL benchmark mSWNoC saves 52.78% for ALASH and 44.94% for AMROOTS of energy with respect to the baseline mesh by incorporating only DTM. When the DTM is enhanced with DVFS the energy savings increases to 70.30% for ALASH and 48.66% for AMROOTS by allowing matching the original latency of the mesh architecture. It can be seen that by incorporating DVFS the energy dissipation advantage ALASH has over AMROOTS grows larger for the CANNEAL benchmark. For all benchmarks considered, ALASH has a lower latency compared to that of AMROOTS. This allows ALASH to have more margin than AMROOTS to match the latency of the original mesh. Hence, it is possible for ALASH to a more aggressive DVFS prediction without introducing latency penalty with respect to the baseline mesh, which in turn saves more energy. It is important to note that performing DTM and DVFS on the mesh architecture does not help in reducing the overall network energy. As the wireline mesh links are highly utilized, there is little opportunity to perform DVFS. For the two benchmarks with lowest switch interaction rates (RADIX and LU), implementing DVFS and DTM on the mesh architecture allows for 10.1% and 4.8% energy savings, respectively, compared to the baseline mesh. In contrast, performing DVFS and DTM on a higher switch interaction rate benchmark like CANNEAL provides a 10.7% energy penalty as the regulator overhead consumes any savings in energy that was possible.

Thermal Characteristics

In this section, we evaluate the thermal profiles of the mSWNoC, SWNoC, and mesh-based architectures employing DTM and DVFS techniques. The focus of this section is to analyze the temperature profiles of the network components. However, we consider the effects of the processing cores in the HotSpot simulation to accurately portray the temperature-coupling effects that the processors have on their nearby network elements.

To evaluate the thermal profile of the network, we consider the improvement of maximum and average switch and link temperatures compared to the baseline mesh as $\Delta T_{\text{hotspot}}$ and ΔT_{avg}, respectively, as the two relevant parameters. Figs. 9.5 and 9.6 show these two parameters for the switches for the various architectures employing the

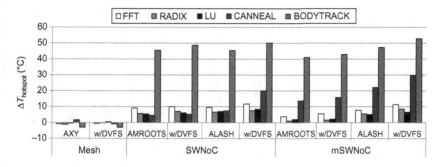

Figure 9.5 Hotspot switch temperature reduction with DTM/DVFS techniques.

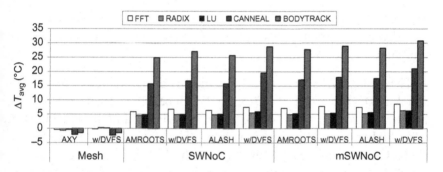

Figure 9.6 Average switch temperature reduction with DTM/DVFS techniques.

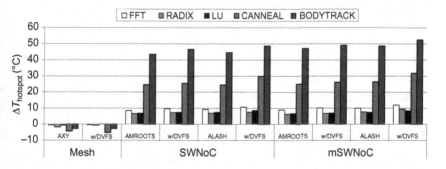

Figure 9.7 Hotspot link temperature reduction with DTM/DVFS techniques.

DTM and DVFS techniques. Figs. 9.7 and 9.8 show these two parameters for the links for the various architectures employing the DTM and DVFS techniques. It can be seen that switches in the mSWNoC architecture are inherently much cooler (positive $\Delta T_{\text{hotspot}}$ and ΔT_{avg}) than the mesh counterpart. From Fig. 9.4, we can see that the difference in energy dissipation between mSWNoC and mesh is significant,

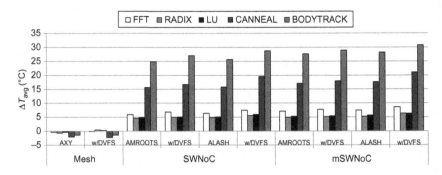

Figure 9.8 Average link temperature reduction with DTM/DVFS techniques.

and hence, it is natural that their switches are cooler. For the same reasons described earlier, the switches are cooler on the mSWNoC when compared to the SWNoC.

The benchmarks vary greatly in the switch interaction rates (injection loads). The FFT, RADIX, and LU benchmarks have very low switch interaction rates. While the CANNEAL and BODYTRACK have higher switch interaction rates than the others. Between the SWNoC and mSWNoC architectures, the SWNoC achieves a higher switch hotspot temperature reduction for the lower switch interaction rate benchmarks, as their traffic density is small. For these benchmarks, the benefits of the wireless shortcuts are outweighed by the amount of traffic that the WIs attract. However, for the higher switch interaction rate benchmarks, the use of high-bandwidth wireless shortcuts, in the mSWNoC, quickly relieves the higher amount of traffic that the WIs attract. In the case of SWNoC, as the shortcuts are implemented through multihop wireline links, moving traffic through these wireline links takes more time and energy which correlates with less temperature reduction.

It can be seen that the switches in the ALASH routing strategy are cooler than their AMROOTS counterpart. This follows the same trend seen in Fig. 9.4, ALASH has less energy dissipation which results in cooler switches. Performing adaptive routing on the mesh architecture is detrimental to the overall temperature profile, as the $\Delta T_{\text{hotspot}}$ and ΔT_{avg} for the majority of the benchmarks are negative (the mesh DTM scheme runs hotter than baseline mesh). As a large region of the mesh network already has hotspot issues, adaptively rerouting traffic through extra hops only expands the hotspot region. However, the original hotspot switch temperature has in fact been reduced by 2.15°C in CANNEAL. However, while reducing the original switch hotspot temperature, a new switch has become hotter. The goal was to decrease the hotspot by routing away from the problem area, and mesh rerouting has infact resulted in the opposite effect.

By performing DVFS on top of the congestion-aware routing schemes, the full thermal profile of ALASH and AMROOTS can be improved significantly. To compare the difference between the two routing strategies with their respective DVFS schemes, the difference in their hotspot temperatures ($\Delta T_{\text{ALASH}-\text{AMROOTS}}$) is considered as the relevant metric. For the switches, $\Delta T_{\text{ALASH}-\text{AMROOTS}}$ is 5.80°C, 7.10°C, 4.30°C, 13.97°C, and 9.87°C for FFT, RADIX, LU, CANNEAL, and BODYTRACK, respectively, when matching the latency of the baseline mesh architecture. Hence, it can be seen that ALASH, while implementing DVFS, performs with less thermal hotspot switches than AMROOTS, as there is a larger margin to perform DVFS. Similar to the switches, the thermal profile of the links of ALASH and AMROOTS can also be improved through the use of DVFS. However, as seen by the switches, ALASH has the opportunity to perform a more aggressive DVFS approach. For the links, $\Delta T_{\text{ALASH}-\text{AMROOTS}}$ is 1.89°C, 2.77°C, 1.57°C, 5.61°C, and 3.38°C for FFT, RADIX, LU, CANNEAL, and BODYTRACK, respectively, at a comparable latency to the baseline mesh architecture.

In the next section, the allowable latency penalty is explored, with respect to mesh, in order to further lower the thermal profiles. Hence, depending on the performance requirements a suitable power–temperature–performance (PTP) trade-off can be established.

Design Space Exploration

As current systems are governed by many requirements of performance, power, heat, etc., there is an onus on the designer to decide what PTP is acceptable. In this respect, the DTM and DVFS algorithms discussed so far can be tuned to specific design requirements. The parameters that provide the optimum energy–delay product for given performance boundaries were found for the benchmarks considered in this work. Fig. 9.9 shows different DVFS operating points (various optimized parameters) for the CANNEAL benchmark as an example. In Fig. 9.9, the latency penalty, energy savings, and

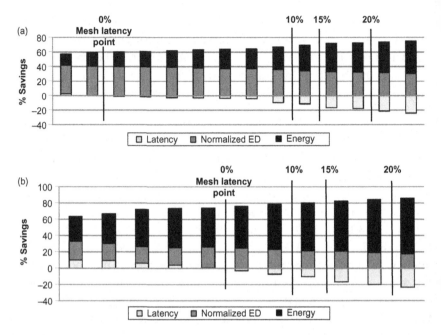

Figure 9.9 Optimizing DVFS window sizes to fit performance boundaries versus mesh for the CANNEAL benchmark for (a) AMROOTS and (b) ALASH.

normalized energy–delay product are shown. In this work, so far we considered choosing the optimized DVFS parameters that provided no latency penalty with respect to the wireline mesh, which were the results presented in earlier parts of this section. Further energy savings, and hence, temperature savings can be obtained by relaxing the acceptable performance boundaries. Given a specific application, a designer may choose an optimum DVFS configuration to suit their performance requirements while minimizing the energy dissipation of the network. From this figure, it can be seen that depending on design requirements, there is an adequate amount of room to obtain a large PTP trade-off. In the CANNEAL benchmark, for example, if a maximum of 20% increase in latency is acceptable, then energy savings can be as much as 72.33%, with a latency penalty of 17.88% with respect to the baseline mesh architecture using the AMROOTS routing and DVFS methodologies. For the ALASH routing and DVFS methodologies that energy savings can increase to 84.12% with a latency penalty of 19.98% with respect to the baseline mesh architecture. Similarly, other trade-off points can be determined for the required PTP target.

Area Overhead

The regulators were chosen for a fully distributed DVFS scheme where each wireline link and switch port has a private regulator (worst case). According to Kim et al. (2008), the regulator area overhead for a single component capable of switching between the six V/F levels was computed to be $0.156\,\text{mm}^2$. By considering a voltage frequency island)–based design, this area overhead can reduced, but is out of the scope of this book (Ogras et al., 2008). Additionally, the hardware overhead for DVFS is shown to be 500 logic gates/switch per port, which is elaborated in Shang et al. (2003). To measure switch and link utilizations, a counter at each output port gathers the total number of cycles that are used to relay flits in each history interval. These counters are reused to monitor switch utilization for DTM, so that it does not introduce any additional area overhead. As this is small compared to the overall switch overhead, it is considered negligible.

REFERENCES

Flich, J., Skeie, T., Mejia, A., Lysne, O., Lopez, P., Robles, A., et al., 2012. A survey and evaluation of topology-agnostic deterministic routing algorithms. IEEE Trans. Parallel Distrib. Syst. 23 (3), 405–425.

Kim, W., Gupta, M., Wei, G.-Y., Brooks, D., 2008. System level analysis of fast, per-core DVFS using on-chip switching regulators. In: Proceedings of the International Symposium on High Performance Computer Architecture. pp. 123–134.

Ogras, U.Y., Marculescu, R., Marculescu, D., 2008.Variation-adaptive feedback control for networks-on-chip with multiple clock domains. In: 45th ACM/IEEE in Design Automation Conference. DAC 2008, 8–13 June 2008. pp. 614–619.

Shang, L., Peh, L.-S., Jha, N.K., 2003. Dynamic voltage scaling with links for power optimization of interconnection networks. In: Proceedings. The Ninth International Symposium on High-Performance Computer Architecture. HPCA-9 2003, 8–12 February 2003. pp. 91–102.

Wettin, P., Murray, J., Pande, P.P., Shirazi, B., Ganguly, A., 2013. Energy-efficient multicore chip design through cross-layer approach. In: Proc. of IEEE Design, Automation, & Test in Europe (DATE).

CHAPTER 10

Conclusions and Possible Future Explorations

The aim of this book has been to demonstrate the potential of wireless small-world Network-on-Chip (NoC) architectures. The architectures proposed and designed, as part of this book, have been demonstrated to deliver superior performance when compared with standard wireline architectures and obtain similar performance with other wireless hierarchical NoCs. The results are promising, and they open up the scope for further research on NoC-based platforms having novel on-chip interconnects and architectures, and distributed cores and memories on a chip. Additionally, to the best of our knowledge, this represents the first comprehensive book undertaken to leverage novel NoC designs as a platform for extensive topology-agnostic dynamic thermal management applications. The need for future research in sophisticated dynamic thermal management (DTM) techniques and NoCs designed with power-management in mind are still required. From this aspect, we present several sections of future work that address our preliminary findings with these two regards.

DESIGN OF 3D WIRELESS SMALL-WORLD NoCs

Three-dimensional (3D) NoCs are also a promising alternative to enhance the performance of multicore chips. Having the extra degree of freedom in the Z-direction promises significant enhancements in both performance and energy dissipation. However, the current 3D architectures that are being tested are all regular in nature, like mesh and different tree structures. Without maximizing the use of the extra Z-direction in 3D NoCs, the enhancements of going 3D will be short lived. Therefore, design of a completely small-world 3D NoC (following the concepts of Chapter 3) is a promising direction. Some recent research in 3D wireless NoC can be found in Matsutani et al. (2013, 2014) and Shamim et al. (2015).

DVFS PRUNING

Depending on the characteristics of the traffic, utilization among the links and switches can vary widely. It has been seen that for some commonly used benchmarks like SPLASH-2 and PARSEC, a majority of links and switches tend to use only a few specific V/F states often, which was shown throughout Chapters 7–9. In this case, a fine-grained DVFS mechanism with many V/F states may be heavily under-utilized, and a DVFS mechanism implemented with a limited number of V/F states may be sufficient. From this preliminary work, we focus on two pruning methodologies to address this concern.

Static Pruning

By eliminating unnecessary V/F states, we can reduce design cost via regulator complexity as well as increase regulator efficiency. Determining which V/F levels to prune and the optimal number of V/F states depend on the characteristics of the traffic and utilization of the switches/links.

The static pruning methodology was created by profiling the energy–delay product (EDP) over each window of T cycles throughout the execution of the benchmark program. For this, the various pruned V/F combinations were tested, and the combinations which provided the minimum EDP over the entire execution of the benchmark were chosen according to,

$$ED_{\min_i} = \min_{\forall x} \frac{\left[\sum_{\forall W_s} ED_i(x)\right]}{N} \qquad (10.1)$$

where $ED_{\min_i}$ is the minimum EDP given i pruned V/F states, $ED_i(x)$ is the EDP when pruning to the V/F state combination x, W_S is a given window, and N is the number of windows over the entire benchmark. In this case (10.1) is obtained by profiling the benchmarks in order to determine the best V/F states to choose. This static pruning methodology requires a priori knowledge of the benchmarks in order to compute the optimal V/F states and categorize the regulator requirements for the benchmarks under consideration. This methodology however may not perform well when previous knowledge of the applications are unknown. Hence, we introduce a dynamic pruning methodology to enhance the EDP of the millimeter-wave SWNoC (mSWNoC) without profiling the benchmarks beforehand.

Dynamic Pruning

In a system that has been implemented with fine-grained DVFS levels, allowing numerous multithreshold jumps (large transitions between voltage states) can lead to significant energy and performance overheads. Similarly, this aggressive DVFS mechanism can lead to significant penalties when wrongly predicting future traffic trends. Instead, choosing opportune times to perform multithreshold jumps should be considered carefully. We develop a machine learning-based approach, adopted from Mitchell (1997) to implement this dynamic pruning. The dynamic pruning methodology consists of three stages: data mining, decision tree, and pruning.

During the data mining stage, the possible pruning decisions are evaluated and a training set of the data is created. After T cycles have elapsed, the traffic utilization, the current V/F pair, and the EDP for the completed portion of the benchmarks are known. Given predictions from the DVFS algorithm for the next window, we can evaluate the EDP gain for every possible pruning decision. This gain is computed using (10.2) with a default pruning configuration which will soon be described

$$ED_{gain}(x) = ED_{prune}(x) - ED_{orig} \tag{10.2}$$

where $ED_{prune}(x)$ is the predicted EDP when pruning to the V/F state combination x, and ED_{orig} is the predicted EDP without pruning. A decision tree is then generated to determine the optimal pruning configuration for the next window period based on the training set data. The data stored in the decision tree is progressively updated with the new ED_{gain} predictions after each window has elapsed, allowing the predictions from the algorithm to improve. The ED_{gain} of each of the decision branches is accumulated and averaged among N window periods, with the most recent window carrying a larger weight. The updated ED_{gain} predictions are computed by

$$ED_{gain}(x, N+1) = ED_{gain}(x, N) + \frac{ED_{gain}(x, N-1)}{W} \tag{10.3}$$

where W is a weight given to the prior ED_{gain} prediction, and ED_{gain} is the EDP for the past $(N-1)$, current (N), or future $(N+1)$ for the given V/F state combination x. In this case, we dynamically adjust the allowable multithreshold jumps based on this decision tree to minimize the predicted EDP of the network. In this regard, the decision tree will choose the path with the largest ED_{gain} shown in (10.4)

$$ED_{\text{maxgain}} = \max_{\forall x}[ED_{\text{gain}}(x, N + 1)] \tag{10.4}$$

and apply the pruning defined by that path for the next window period. A tree of depth three was created consisting of two subtrees which split (10.2) into either a positive or negative ED_{gain}. The negative subtree $(-)$ can be ignored as we are attempting to maximize the EDP gain. The two levels in the positive subtree $(+)$ consist of the V/F combinations as a first-level attribute and the pruning configuration as a second-level attribute. An example of this pruning decision tree is shown in Fig. 10.1. For instance, let us assume that the fine-grained DVFS mechanism has four V/F states, V_1, V_2, V_3, and V_4, respectively. Here, choosing to remove either V_2 or V_3 would result in a positive ED_{gain}. Hence, it is predicted that by removing one of these two states, there will be an improvement to the EDP. At the second level, the configuration determines the behavior of the pruned state in the DVFS mechanism. As an example, by removing V_2 as shown by the left most branch of Fig. 10.1, there are two other possible configurations when the base DVFS algorithm selects V_2. Here, we can either tune to the next available lower or higher state. Based on these two levels in the positive subtree, the path that maximizes the ED_{gain} defined in (10.4) is chosen, and the states are pruned accordingly.

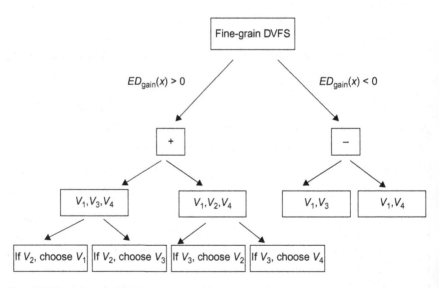

Figure 10.1 Example pruning decision tree.

Voltage Regulator Characteristics

The efficiency and transient response of a regulator directly impacts the performance of a DVFS algorithm. Traditionally, there are three main types of regulators: linear regulators, switched capacitor (SC) regulators, and switched inductor (SI) regulators. All of them have their own advantages and disadvantages when being used as a regulator for DVFS. For example, linear regulators and SI regulators are capable of supporting fine-grained DVFS; however, the efficiency of linear regulators drops as its output voltage decreases, and SI regulators require high-quality inductors, which are difficult to efficiently integrate on chip. Meanwhile, SC regulators are better suited for coarse-grained DVFS with two or three voltage levels as higher number of levels increase the design complexity and degrade efficiency. For our investigation, we developed a hybrid regulator, which combines the characteristics of an SC regulator and an SI regulator to bring out the advantages of both while alleviating their disadvantages. Since a smaller inductor is more efficiently integrated on chip, and in the hybrid switched inductor switched capacitor (SISC) regulator design, the inductor is placed on top of the capacitors which are implemented by MOSFET capacitors; the result is a compact and efficient integrated regulator which is capable of supporting a fine- or course-grained DVFS algorithm. The details of this regulator's design are out of the scope of this chapter.

In this chapter nominal range operation is considered. Hence, the adopted DVFS strategy uses discrete V/F pairs that maintain a linear relationship. The initial fine-grained levels are: 1 V/2.5 GHz, 0.9 V/2.25 GHz, 0.8 V/2.0 GHz, 0.7 V/1.75 GHz, 0.6 V/1.5 GHz, and 0.5 V/1.25 GHz. The voltage regulator was designed in TSMC 65-nm CMOS process and simulated in Cadence Analog Design Environment. Table 10.1 shows the timing, efficiency, and energy overhead for switching between voltages for the designed regulator. The efficiency is higher for larger output voltage as power loss becomes smaller relative to the output power. The switch time (the transient time between two voltage levels) depends on the initial voltage and the final voltage rather than the step size. Also, the efficiency and switch time are different between the step-up and step-down cases. During step-up, power is drawn from the supply through the low-resistance switches to charge the capacitor, but during step-down, the capacitor is mainly discharged through the load.

Table 10.1 Voltage Regulator Timing and Efficiency Step-Up (Step-Down) Characteristics

V_1	0.5					0.6				0.7			0.8		0.9
V_2	0.6	0.7	0.8	0.9	1.0	0.7	0.8	0.9	1.0	0.8	0.9	1.0	0.9	1.0	1.0
Switch Time (ns)	16 (21)	27 (34)	30 (35)	30 (35)	18 (33)	17 (26)	30 (39)	25 (43)	20 (38)	13 (19)	16 (14)	12 (24)	15 (15)	11 (19)	15 (18)
Efficiency (%)	53.7 (56.0)	49.9 (64.0)	51.2 (65.7)	49.2 (64.7)	46.2 (66.5)	55.6 (68.5)	53.7 (67.4)	54.1 (66.0)	47.6 (68.9)	56.9 (61.1)	60.5 (69.7)	54.1 (66.5)	61.2 (66.7)	56.0 (72.8)	65.7 (66.0)
Energy Overhead (nJ)	0.10 (0.10)	0.24 (0.17)	0.38 (0.27)	0.57 (0.40)	0.81 (0.50)	0.12 (0.08)	0.26 (0.18)	0.41 (0.31)	0.67 (0.40)	0.13 (0.12)	0.25 (0.19)	0.47 (0.34)	0.13 (0.11)	0.32 (0.20)	0.13 (0.13)

DVFS Pruning Setup

Several relevant constraints need to be determined for the DVFS pruning algorithm to ensure that the achievable performance in the presence of DVFS with or without pruning remains nearly the same. In this regard, we never prune the V_{dd} state (highest voltage level) and limit the maximum number of pruned states to be 3 (in this case half of the total number of initial states). With more aggressive pruning, say only two states left, there is little room to catch moderately utilized links and either a hefty performance penalty will be applied, or a large amount of energy is unnecessarily wasted. Hence, by keeping a minimum number of three states, we can match or exceed the EDP of the fine-grained DVFS mechanism with an original six states. Additionally, modifying the DVFS behavior with pruned states is essential to maintain the achievable gain in EDP. These behaviors are shown as the second level of the positive subtree in Fig. 10.1, and can be categorized into three main steps:

1. See if the next highest V/F state is available.
2. If not, go back to the previous state.
3. If also not available, go to the next lowest state.

The various behaviors can be any permutation of the three steps described above with the default sequence being (1, 2, 3), to achieve energy saving without paying a large penalty. The selected behavior can vary between each window period for each benchmark as well, and is chosen to maximize the ED_{gain}.

Performance Evaluation of Static DVFS Pruning

In this section, we present the latency and network-level energy dissipation of the mSWNoC by incorporating the statically pruned DVFS technique described earlier. For completeness, we also show the characteristics of the conventional wireline mesh architecture incorporating the DVFS and pruned DVFS techniques. We have enhanced this work with several more benchmarks from the PARSEC suite as well.

To determine the appropriate number of pruned V/F levels, we first obtain the minimum EDPs from (10.1). For analysis we ranged the number of pruned states from 0 to 3. Fig. 10.2a shows that depending on the benchmark, pruning several states does not affect the performance. In fact, in certain cases, it can even help to reduce the EDP further. The optimal number of pruned states varies among the 10 benchmarks as shown in Fig. 10.2a. The benchmarks can be classified into three categories

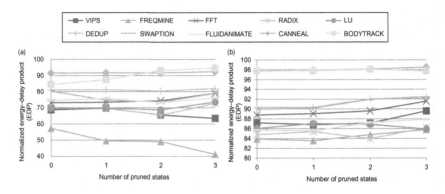

Figure 10.2 Effects of static DVFS pruning on (a) mSWNoC and (b) mesh architectures.

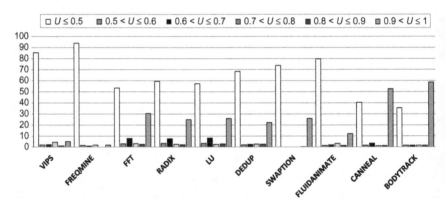

Figure 10.3 Histogram of wireline link utilization on mSWNoC.

depending on their link utilizations, which can be seen in Fig. 10.3 and the number of V/F states necessary for optimum EDP.

Benchmarks with low utilization (VIPS, FREQMINE): These benchmarks work well with a course-grained DVFS mechanism and can be pruned down to 3 *V/F* levels. As an example, FREQMINE has over 90% of the wireline links operating below 50% utilization, which can be seen in Fig. 10.3. In this case, we can prune many of the central states without paying large penalties to either energy or latency.

Benchmarks with moderate utilization (FFT, RADIX, LU, DEDUP, SWAPTION, FLUIDANIMATE): these benchmarks work well with a semicourse-grained DVFS mechanism and can be pruned down to 4 *V/F* levels. With the exception of FFT (pruned to five levels), all of the benchmarks in this classification achieve better EDP than without pruning.

Benchmarks with high utilization (CANNEAL, BODYTRACK): These benchmarks do not work well with pruning. BODYTRACK as an example has a more even distribution of V/F usage among the links. In BODYTRACK as an example 60% of the wireline links fall above 90% utilization. In this case, if we prune the central V/F states, we will lose opportunities to tune the V/F state to an appropriate level. Also, there is a higher probability of paying a large penalty if mispredictions occur. In this case, it is clear from Fig. 10.2a, that fine-grained V/F levels are more appropriate and hence pruning states increases the overall EDP.

In Fig. 10.2b it is evident that performing fine-grained DVFS is necessary, and pruning will mostly hurt the EDP for the mesh architecture. This is due to the fact that the wireline mesh links are highly utilized, as shown in Fig. 10.3. On the mSWNoC architecture, wireline link utilizations are heavily reduced due to a reduction in hop count as well as a significant amount of traffic traversing the energy-efficient wireless channels. This reduction in wireline link utilization facilitates DVFS on them, while the mesh does not have the same architectural benefits.

Fig. 10.4a and b shows the latency and network energy dissipation for the various architectures, respectively. While determining the overall network latency, we incorporated the additional delay introduced by the synchronization circuits required for data traversals between various V/F levels (Beer et. al, 2010). It can be observed from Fig. 10.4a that for all of the benchmarks considered, the latency of the base mSWNoC is lower than that of the mesh architecture. This is due to the small-world architecture of mSWNoC with direct long-range, one-hop wireless links that enables a smaller average hop count than that of mesh. However, it should be noted that in the presence of DVFS the latency for both mesh and mSWNoC increase slightly.

Fig. 10.4b shows the normalized total network energy dissipation for the mSWNoC and mesh architectures. It can be observed from Fig. 10.4b that in each benchmark, the network energy is much lower for the mSWNoC compared to the mesh architecture. The two main contributors of the energy dissipation are the switches and the interconnect infrastructure. In the mSWNoC, the overall switch energy decreases significantly compared to a mesh as a result of the better connectivity of the architecture. In this case, the hop count decreases significantly, and hence, on the average, packets have to traverse through less number of switches and links. In addition, a significant

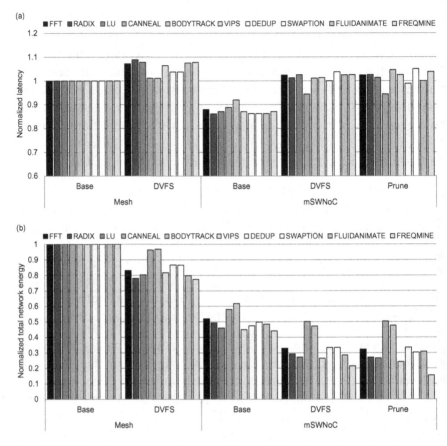

Figure 10.4 (a) Normalized average network latency and (b) normalized total network energy for static pruning.

amount of traffic traverses through the energy-efficient wireless channels in mSWNoC, consequently allowing the interconnect energy dissipation of mSWNoC to further decrease compared to the mesh. With the addition of DVFS, the total network energy can be further reduced. As the traffic traversing through the wireline links is heavily reduced in the mSWNoC, the opportunity for implementing DVFS is significant. Hence, though DVFS introduces slight latency degradation, the overall EDP improves significantly.

From Fig. 10.4b, it is clear that for the FREQMINE benchmark, as an example, mSWNoC saves 55.9% of energy compared to the baseline mesh, and when enhanced with DVFS the energy savings increases to 78.6%. Furthermore, by performing pruning on the DVFS, the energy savings can be increased to 84.7% with only an additional 1.3%

increase in latency. In these circumstances, we are only showing the pruned DVFS that minimized the EDP. In the FREQMINE benchmark, the EDP was reduced after pruning three states, which were 0.5, 0.7, and 0.8 V. After removing these states, a large voltage gap has been created as described earlier. In this scenario, the regulator design allows for these larger jumps (between 0.6 and 0.9 V) without significant performance or energy impacts when the DVFS prediction does not vary drastically between nearby windows. Similarly, choosing a lower V/F of 0.6 V for the removed states has further improved energy without a high latency penalty (as the EDP has been reduced). It is important to note that performing DVFS on the mesh architecture also helps to reduce the energy dissipation by 22.58% for FREQMINE without pruning. Pruning on the mesh architecture in all benchmarks does not reduce the EDP though. As the wireline mesh links are highly utilized, there is less opportunity to perform DVFS and an even smaller opportunity to prune the V/F states.

Performance Evaluation of Dynamic DVFS Pruning

In this section, we present the benefits of a dynamic pruning methodology to improve the energy of a base DVFS methodology without the need to profile the benchmarks necessary to implement the static pruning. Fig. 10.5 shows the comparison between the base DVFS strategy on the mSWNoC architecture in the presence of static pruning, multithreshold jump, and dynamic pruning approaches. We consider the EDP as the relevant parameter. The latency penalty for the multithreshold jump and static/dynamic pruning methods were matched with the original penalty introduced by the base DVFS methodology. From

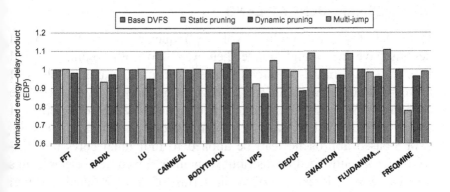

Figure 10.5 Normalized EDP with respect to baseline DVFS on mSWNoC.

Fig. 10.5, it can be seen that for nearly all of the benchmarks, the dynamic pruning methodology outperforms the base and multithreshold jump DVFS strategies. The regulator switching times shown in Table 10.1 demonstrates that multithreshold jumps are possible without introducing a large time penalty. Thus, the benefit of switching between far-apart states is limited to the accuracy of the underlying DVFS mechanism. It is clear that by allowing any multithreshold jumps, the EDP is increased for many of the benchmarks. This is due to the potentially large overhead in energy when the regulators switch frequently over large voltage ranges. By dynamically pruning, we can pick opportune moments to perform multithreshold jumps, to enhance the EDP. For the most part, the dynamic pruning methodology, using no a priori knowledge of the benchmark traffic can provide similar improvement of EDP over the original DVFS mechanism when compared to the static pruning methodology. In the best case (VIPS), by adding this dynamic pruning methodology on top of the base DVFS algorithm, we can reduce the EDP by an additional 13.1% without incurring any additional latency penalty with respect to the original DVFS. The static pruning method reduces EDP by 7.7% with respect to the original DVFS. As dynamic pruning allows for adjustments to required levels over time, the EDP can be further improved over the static methodology. If the multithreshold jump methodology is used, the overall EDP is increased by an additional 5% instead. The only benchmark that performed worse (larger EDP than the base DVFS) with the dynamic pruning methodology was BODYTRACK. In this scenario, as mentioned earlier, there is little opportunity for pruning as the link utilizations are high for this benchmark.

VOLTAGE FREQUENCY ISLAND

In the last few years, multiple voltage frequency island (VFI)−based designs have increasingly made their way into both commercial and research platforms. NoC architectures partitioned into multiple VFI are capable of minimizing energy dissipation subject to performance constraints. With this architecture, it becomes possible to do efficient power and thermal management of multicore platforms via DVFS. DVFS-based approaches can be applied to individual cores independently, in a centralized or distributed manner. From our research thus far, we have addressed DVFS in terms of a distributed fashion. However, research should be done to analyze the benefits of performing a course-grain approach in terms of the level of DVFS. There is a need to ensure the system is not overdesigned, and as such simple regulators as well as course-grain approaches (requiring fewer regulators) should be explored.

Toward this end, most of the existing VFI-partitioned designs principally use the conventional multihop mesh-based NoC architecture, limitations of which are well known. However, it has been already shown that small-world network architectures with long-range wireless shortcuts can significantly improve the energy consumption and achievable data rates of massive multicore-based computing platforms (Deb et al., 2010). Hence coupling these techniques with state-of-the-art interconnect infrastructures is the key for future sustainable many-core architectures.

CONCLUDING REMARKS

It is clear that there is a significant need to further study the power−temperature−performance trade-offs for future many-core NoC systems. This book was to the best of our knowledge the first comprehensive book undertaken to leverage novel NoC designs as a platform for extensive topology-agnostic dynamic thermal management applications. By performing joint DTM and DVFS on an mSWNoC, we have demonstrated significant sustainability in terms of thermal and energy improvement without performance degradation compared to the traditional mesh-based NoC architecture.

REFERENCES

Beer, S., et al., 2010. The devolution of synchronizers. In: Proc. of ASYNC.

Deb, S., et al., 2010. Enhancing performance of network-on-chip architectures with millimeter-wave wireless interconnects. In: IEEE International Conference on Application-Specific Systems, Architectures and Processors (ASAP), pp. 73−80.

Matsutani, H., et al., 2013. A case for wireless 3D NoCs for CMPs. In: Proceedings of DAC, pp. 23−28.

Matsutani, H., et al., 2014. Low-latency wireless 3D NoCs via randomized shortcut chips. In: Proceedings of DATE, pp. 1−6.

Mitchell, T., 1997. Decision tree learning. In: Mitchell, T. (Ed.), Machine Learning. The McGraw-Hill Companies, Inc., New York, NY, pp. 52−78.

Shamim, M., et al., 2015. Co-design of 3D wireless Network-on-Chip architectures with microchannel-based cooling. In: Proceedings of IGSC, pp. 1−6.

Printed in the United States
By Bookmasters